P9-CFP-950

WITHDRAWN

The Story of

SEEDS

The Story of
SEEDS

FROM MENDEL'S GARDEN TO YOUR PLATE, AND HOW
THERE'S MORE OF LESS TO EAT AROUND THE WORLD

Nancy F. Castaldo

HOUGHTON MIFFLIN HARCOURT
Boston   New York

Text copyright
© 2016 by Nancy F. Castaldo // All
rights reserved. For information about per-
mission to reproduce selections from this book,
write to Permissions, Houghton Mifflin Harcourt
Publishing Company, 215 Park Avenue South, New York,
New York 10003. // All photos by Nancy F. Castaldo except
p. i (corn) Siede Preis/Getty Images; pp. iii, 115–19 (sprouts)
Filipe B. Varela/Shutterstock; p. iv, v (dirt + sprout) Organics
Media Library/Alamy; p. vii (oak leaf) Alistair Scott/Alamy; pp.
1 and throughout (sunflower seed pile) Igor Dutina/iStockphoto;
pp. 7, 11, 16 (stamps from author's collection); p. 14 Lucie A.
Castaldo (photo of author); p. 30 Dr. Luigi Guarino; p. 36,
47–48 Library of Congress; pp. 121–22 (pod) Lepas2004/
iStockphoto; p. 123 (soybean seeds) Photodisc/Getty
Images // www.hmhco.com // The text of this book is
set in Adobe Garamond Pro. // ISBN 978-0-544-
32023-9 // Manufactured in China //
SCP 10 9 8 7 6 5 4 3 2 1
4500558674

TO ALL
THE "SEEDY" FOLKS
I'VE ENCOUNTERED
IN THE BUCKET
BRIGADE!

—N.F.C.

To see
things in the seed,
that is genius.

—Lao Tzu

Contents

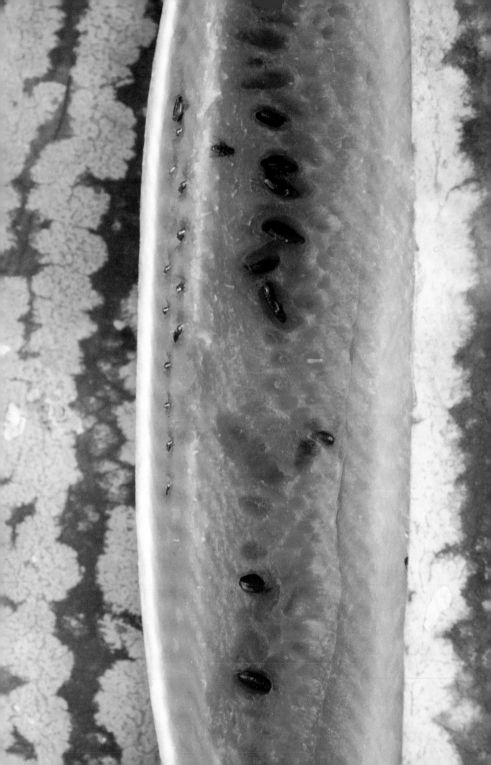

CHAPTER ONE

SEEDS AT RISK

Y ou spit a watermelon seed onto your plate, wishing your slice were seedless. You flick the black dots into the trash before loading the dishwasher. They're garbage, right?

But what if your sweet slice were from the very last watermelon in the world? Would you still spit out the seeds into the trash—or would you risk your life to save each one? Fortunately, you don't have to make that choice and watermelons are not crucial to our survival, not even on a hot day. But what if it weren't watermelons that were threatened? What if it were one of our priority crops, like wheat, corn, rice, or potatoes? What if you were facing a great famine, like they did in Ireland? Now the stakes would be higher. Would you face danger to save any of their seeds?

We're in the midst of a seed crisis. Every day new headlines jump at us. Seeds are facing many threats. And when they are threatened, our food supply is also at risk.

It may sound crazy, even improbable, but there are scientists who are risking their lives every day for seeds. It's true, and they've been doing it for years.

Scientists, such as the Russian seed collector Nikolai Vavilov, have recognized the importance of seeds and have given their lives to protect one of our planet's greatest treasures. There are people throughout the world who are striving to defend and protect our seeds. Some plant them. Some share them. Some smuggle them. Some save them. All are working toward keeping the diversity of our seeds alive and well.

I

Field corn harvest.

SEED CRISIS

Although war takes its toll on agriculture and seeds, it isn't the only challenge facing them. Climate change, overexploitation, bioterrorism, and modern agriculture practices are threatening our seeds and decreasing our agricultural biological diversity (agrobiodiversity).

According to the Food and Agriculture Organization (FAO) of the United Nations, some 75 percent of plant genetic diversity has been lost since the 1900s because farmers have chosen to abandon their local crop species for genetically uniform, high-yielding ones. More than 90 percent of crop varieties are no longer being farmed.

Of 300,000 species of edible plants, only about 150 to 200

are being cultivated, only eight are traded throughout the world, and half of our calories come from just three — rice, maize, and wheat. According to the Global Crop Diversity Trust, 23 percent of the calories we live on and consume in every country comes from wheat. Our diversity is shrinking fast. The world's seeds are in crisis.

SCIENTISTS RISK LIVES, EARN AWARD

The scientists of Syria's ICARDA gene-bank received the prestigious Gregor Mendel Award in March of 2015 for risking their lives to preserve almost 150,000 seed samples during the civil war in Syria. Most of those samples are safe at the Svalbard Global Seed Vault now!

Small farmers struggle against large farms.

CHAPTER TWO

SEED PIONEERS

Any dictionary can provide you with the definition of a seed. It's a small object that is produced by a plant so that a new plant can grow. But that definition doesn't begin to describe how important these tiny little objects are and why people have been willing to protect them.

A seed holds all the genetic information for a plant. Many seeds can be eaten just as they are, like corn and chestnuts. Others are planted and provide us with the fruits, vegetables, and medicines we need to survive. Those plants help maintain our atmosphere. They take in carbon dioxide and provide us with the oxygen we breathe. In addition, think of all the creatures that also need seeds or the plants they produce to survive.

SEED
Similar to an egg, a seed or kernel is covered by a seed coat for protection and houses a fertilized plant ovule that contains a tiny embryonic plant and nutrition.

Seeds equal life.

Thousands of years ago, humans were hunter-gatherers. Although there were hundreds of thousands of fresh fruits, nuts, vegetables, and grains growing at that time, we would hardly recognize many of them. Take corn, for example. It wasn't always the tasty cob treat we eat today. It started out as just a single kernel wrapped in its own husk.

The domestication that began with the sowing of seeds moved humans away from hunting and gathering and into harvesting.

4

Chestnuts in their prickly husks.

Most of the seeds that existed then had adapted to breaking open and dropping to the ground with a breeze or a brush of an animal's tail. The plant's survival depended on its ability to spread its seeds.

But humans changed that when they began to harvest and plant. They gathered seeds that remained on the plants and were able to be collected. Season after season humans planted and harvested.

After many, many years those seeds became the domesticated varieties we have today, and they are genetically different from their wild counterparts.

The ancient art of growing food from seeds has undergone many changes. Family farming has developed into a large, mechanized, high-tech business with emphasis on feeding growing populations. How did agriculture become what it is today?

Early farm at the Farmer's Museum in Cooperstown, New York.

Let's take a look back at a few of the pioneers who gave us the fundamentals of the science of agriculture.

GREGOR MENDEL, THE MONK IN THE GARDEN

Humans have been creating variations of plants for hundreds of years. It all started with peas. Do you have your mom's eyes? Or your father's dark hair? We don't give a second thought to accepting the principles of inheritance. We now know that we have genes that carry traits from parent to child, but inheritance was once a mystery. We can thank a nineteenth-century monk by the name of Gregor Mendel for our early knowledge of genetics.

Mendel was born Johann Mendel on July 22, 1822, on his family's farm in what was then Austria. He excelled at school and following his graduation went on to study physics and math. His father expected him to return to the family farm after graduation, but instead Mendel joined the Augustinian order of monks at Saint Thomas's Abbey in Brno and was given the name Gregor.

The monastery did not shut him out from the world, but rather enlightened him through its extensive library and the research and teaching of its monks. He furthered his studies of mathematics and physics under the direction of Christian Doppler, and also began studies in botany at the University of Vienna. When he returned to the monastery he taught and began to conduct his own research.

And Mendel did not stray too far from farming. He chose to work with peas in the monastery garden of Saint Thomas's Abbey. They were perfect for his research because peas are able to pollinate themselves. The anthers holding the pollen and the stigma, which receives the pollen, are enclosed in an envelope of petals, preventing outside pollination by insects and wind. This is why pea plants are exactly like their parent plants. This is also why it was relatively easy for Mendel to conduct his experiments between 1856 and 1863.

SELF-POLLINATE
To transfer pollen from the anther to the stigma in the same flower.

Mendel acted as the breeder for his pea plants. Using tweezers, he gently pulled back the petals and introduced pollen from a different plant to the exposed stigma. Then he tied a little sack around each flower to prevent any further pollination by insects or wind to the now exposed stigma. He selected pea plants based on their different traits. He studied pod color, pod shape, plant height, flower color, flower position, pea color, and pea shape.

For example, in describing the variations in pod shape, Gregor Mendel wrote in 1865, "To the difference in the form of the ripe pods. These are either simply inflated, not contracted in places; or they are deeply constricted between the seeds and more or less wrinkled (*P. saccharatum*)."

The offspring of two plants he bred were hybrids. He found that they had traits from both of the pea plant parents. Even though Mendel created these hybrids himself, hybrids usually occur naturally through cross-pollination.

Mendel conducted experiments with peas for eight years, with over ten thousand pea plants. He published his results in 1865. He found seven dominant traits in the first generation of hybrid

pea plants, which included "the simply inflated form of the pod."

Not all plants pass on their genes exactly as Mendel's peas did, but many do show the same patterns of inheritance.

Mendel's discoveries and the laws of inheritance he developed were not well received or appreciated during his lifetime. For the most part, they were misunderstood to be writings about science that was already known. They were not recognized for the revolutionary ideas they were bringing forth.

HYBRID

First- or second-generation cross of inbred parent lines. Offspring seeds will not exhibit the traits of the parents, or breed true. Instead, they will take on some or none of their genetic traits; e.g., a poodle and a golden retriever will not produce a poodle. They will produce a goldendoodle.

Pea plants at a community garden.

MENDEL'S LAWS
OF HEREDITY

1. **Law of segregation: A pair of genes defines each inherited trait, such as eye color. Offspring inherit one genetic allele from each parent.**
2. **Law of independent assortment: Since genes are sorted separately from each other, the inheritance of one trait is not dependent on the inheritance of another.**
3. **Law of dominance: An organism with alternate forms of a gene will express the dominant gene.**

This did not seem to discourage the scientist monk, who was reported to have shared his feelings with Abbot Barina, who was the last novice Mendel accepted into the monastery: "Though I have had to live through many bitter moments in my life, I must admit with gratitude that the beautiful and good prevailed. My scientific work brought me much satisfaction, and I am sure it will soon be recognized by the whole world."

Fortunately, scientists took another look at Mendel's findings in 1900, and his work in genetics was finally appreciated. The foundation is all that remains of the greenhouse where Mendel bred his peas, but scientists still use his principles to explain heredity. Farmers and horticulturists like pioneering botanist Luther Burbank use them as they cross species to achieve desirable traits in their produce. They might cross two parent plants to achieve a bigger or sweeter fruit, or a plant that resists a disease.

ALLELES
Multiple forms of genes on a chromosome.

LUTHER BURBANK, PLANT WIZARD

Far away from the walled gardens of Mendel's abbey, Luther Burbank's gardens and house sit like a memorial to the genius who once lived on a street corner in Santa Rosa, California. A white picket fence surrounds the property. Following in the footsteps of Helen Keller, Henry Ford, Jack London, and so many others who came to see the Plant Wizard, you walk through the gate. You see roses to the left, a flower border and green lawns to the right. Underneath that lawn, where a cedar tree once grew, is the unmarked grave of the man who drew so many to his gardens.

You walk past the old, fire-scarred walnut tree that has witnessed every visitor and follow the path to the gardens behind the house. You stop short. A giant cactus plant, the size of a two-car garage, dominates the gardens. Wow! You don't know much about Luther Burbank, but figure he must have loved cacti. And you're right.

Burbank grew up loving plants. In fact, he had a pet cactus that he carried around just like a doll when he was a little boy. That early relationship influenced his decision to create the massive plant that grows before you.

He was born in Lancaster, Massachusetts, the thirteenth child in his family. Burbank didn't have a strong formal education, but he read. He became inspired by Darwin's 1868 book *Variations of Animals and Plants Under Domestication*. It led him to his first experiment—an attempt to create a new variety of potato in 1873.

Burbank's giant cactus still grows at the Luther Burbank Home and Gardens in Santa Rosa, California.

That plant, which became known as the Burbank potato, launched his career. In fact, it is the potato that made McDonald's fries so famous. The sale of the rights to the potato brought Burbank $150 and the opportunity to move to California, where the growing season far exceeds the one in New England.

By crossing and recrossing unusual species of plants, known as novelties, Burbank introduced desirable characteristics into common varieties. He even developed the giant cactus that dominates his garden to this very day! That big old cactus actually consists of seven different species of prickly pear cacti, including varieties of the nonprickly, or spineless, pear cactus that Burbank created. It took Burbank over twenty years to develop the spineless

FAST FOOD FRIES

McDonald's buys more than 3.4 billion pounds (1.5 billion kilograms) of potatoes from American farmers each year. They have been planting the Russet Burbank for years, although they would prefer it to mature sooner, use less water, and be hardier. Still, Idaho farmers cite that in 2008, 57 percent of their acreage was planted with the Burbank.

cactus. Between 1907 and 1925, he introduced more than sixty different varieties. He wanted to develop a cactus that could be used to feed cattle. It sold very successfully at first, with flat, hand-sized oval pads (also called thalli) of the cactus selling for up to $1,000 each, a tremendous amount of money in those days. But the success didn't last. The cattle found the prickly pear so tasty that they didn't just munch it; they devoured the entire cactus, making the plant economically unfeasible for ranchers to replenish.

Burbank created more than eight hundred new vegetables, fruits, and flowers, many of which are quite common today, such as the Satsuma plum, elephant garlic, the Shasta daisy, the plumcot, and a variety of different walnuts. He showed the world that plants can be altered and created to suit our needs. It's no wonder people called him the Plant Wizard.

Luther Burbank sold his seeds from this little building attached to his house.

CACTUS PADS

THE FLAT, OVAL PADS, or thalli, that grow from the prickly pear cactus are its leaves. A new plant can be grown from one pad by placing the pad upright with its lower one-third in sandy, well-drained soil.

I was given one of Burbank's cactus pads when I visited. After a full year it finally sprouted! We thought it was going to die and imagined the early farmers paying so much for each precious pad.

Prickly pear cactus pads should be placed in a sunny spot and should not be watered until new green growth develops. Watering should then be limited to infrequent deep soakings, to allow the soil to dry out in between. The plant can be kept in a container, but eventually it should be given more growing room outdoors (if you live in a warm climate!).

A single cactus pad.

A planted cactus pad with new growth.

PLANT PATENT

LUTHER BURBANK DID NOT RECEIVE the first plant patent, nor did he receive any while he was alive. His book *How Plants Are Treated to Work for Man*, however, influenced the development of the plant patent in 1930. In support of the legislation for the patent, inventor Thomas Edison testified before Congress, "This [bill] will, I feel sure, give us many more Burbanks."

The first patent went to Henry Boseberg in 1931 for his climbing, ever-blooming rose. According to the patent law, a plant patent is issued to a person who "first appreciates the distinctive qualities of a plant and reproduces it asexually" (by grafting or breeding). A patent cannot be granted to someone who discovers a plant in the wild that can occur freely in nature, nor can one be issued for a plant produced by seed.

Plant elements, such as genes, DNA, pollen, and plant-based chemicals, now fall under a different patent called a utility patent. In this case, the plant element must be made by humans. A purchaser of a patented seed under this law cannot manufacture the seed line. (There's more about this in the next chapter!)

Plant Wizard Luther Burbank was given sixteen patents for his plant varieties after his death.

35 U.S. CODE § 161—PATENTS FOR PLANTS

"Whoever invents or discovers and asexually reproduces any distinct and new variety of plant, including cultivated sports [part of a woody plant, also referred to as a bud sport], mutants, hybrids, and newly found seedlings, other than a tuber propagated plant or a plant found in an uncultivated state, may obtain a patent therefore, subject to the conditions and requirements of this title. The provisions of this title relating to patents for inventions shall apply to patents for plants, except as otherwise provided."

NIKOLAI VAVILOV — WORLD EXPLORER AND FOUNDING FATHER OF SEED COLLECTING

Professor Igor Luskutov opens the door to Nikolai Vavilov's office at the Vavilov Research Institute of Plant Industry in Saint Petersburg, Russia. Years after Vavilov's death, the office looks as if the world-renowned scientist just left—perhaps stepped out for a cup of tea, or went away on a seed-collecting trip. His phone and inkwells are at the ready on his desk, and a map of his expeditions lies flat under a sheet of Plexiglas. Like so many seed scientists who have made the pilgrimage to this museum space within the institute, I stand in awe of where Vavilov commanded such a presence.

Born in Russia in 1887, Vavilov was known for his remarkable memory, a great trait for someone interested in seed science and plants. But he didn't begin his career with plants. Since his father was a successful merchant, he entered a business school before pursuing his agricultural studies.

He left Russia in 1916 on his first major expedition to collect seeds in northern Persia (now Iran) for the Persian imperial army, and then to the Pamirs, a steep mountain range in Central Asia in what is now Tajikistan, for the Russian Ministry of Agriculture.

Vavilov's desk still sits in his office in Russia.

The narrow trails and rocky ledges of the Pamirs made it difficult for travelers, especially pack horses. The party couldn't travel more than a mile an hour. The expedition, like so many others Vavilov took, was risky. The places he visited were not welcoming and certainly not safe for outsiders, especially in the third year of World War I. Fighting was all around them. This trip was marked with disaster when Cossacks, sent by the Russian tsar to retrieve tribesmen who had fled into the Pamirs, attacked Vavilov and his companions. Vavilov was deserted by his guides and arrested as a spy for Germany upon his return to Russia. But that didn't stop him. The rye, wheat, lentil, and other seeds he collected at great risk became the start of the seed bank at the Department of Applied Botany in Leningrad, which would later be known as the Nikolai Ivanovich Vavilov All-Russian Research Institute of Plant Industry (N.I. Vavilov Research Institute of Plant Industry).

BOTANY
The scientific study
of plants.

17

Although seeds had been collected before for plant-breeding programs, Vavilov was one of the first scientists to collect seeds for conservation. He told his Leningrad (now Saint Petersburg) staff in 1923 that their task was not only to gather plants for breeding, but also to save seeds from extinction. Those were very strong words in 1923, but not loud enough to sound the alarm across the world.

One of Vavilov's friends, the American plant breeder and agronomist Harry Harlan, was one of the only scientists who also recognized that modern agricultural practices were beginning to threaten important domesticated crop species with extinction. It was a very disturbing revelation.

Vavilov spent the rest of his life traveling from country to country on seed collection expeditions—sixty-four in total on five continents. He even visited the United States, where he visited with Luther Burbank and set up the New York Division of the Department of Applied Botany and Plant Breeding. Throughout his travels he collected seeds for Russia, but it wasn't always easy. Permissions were difficult to obtain. Seed collecting and exploration were dangerous business. He encountered bandits, suffered from typhus during his 1927 expedition to Ethiopia, and fell ill with malaria in Syria.

Vavilov was a true visionary. In 1926 he published his theory of "centers of diversity" (also known as centers of origin). According to Vavilov's principle, the area where a plant was first domesticated is where the greatest number of strains of the plant can be found. Vavilov mapped out the distribution of diversity throughout the world. He was able to determine where crops originated. And he realized that the longer a crop had been grown, the more diversity it would reveal.

"Knowledge of the basic function of the universal agricultural centers throws light on the entire history of mankind as well as the history of common crops," wrote Vavilov in his 1926 book, *Origin and Geography of Cultivated Plants.*

He agreed with the beliefs of his hero, Charles Darwin, whose portrait still hangs above the fireplace in Vavilov's office. Darwin's theory of the origin of species was in line with Vavilov's theory on the "centers of origin." He believed that "botanists, zoologists, geneticists, plant breeders and ecologists as well as plant geographers" should be influenced by Darwin's theory of evolution.

Vavilov had been born to a wealthy merchant. For most people, this would have proved advantageous, but not for him. Although he was well educated, his background proved to further his challenges after Stalin came to power in 1922. Russians of peasant stock, like Vavilov's scientific rival Trofim Lysenko, gained esteem, while people like Vavilov became distrusted and despised by the new Bolshevik administration. Not only did he come from an upper class, but he also had the privilege of being educated in both England and America before the revolution of 1917. "He does not claim, as Lysenko does, that Communism has done everything for him," said British botanist J. G. Hawkes.

Native corn from Vavilov's expedition to South America on display in his office in Russia.

Lysenko did not agree with Darwin's theories or Mendel's principles. Instead, he proposed quick crop improvements based on Jean-Baptiste Lamarck's genetic theories that focused on the belief that acquired traits could be passed on to offspring. He attacked Vavilov's Mendelian scientific principles. Stalin, a supporter of Lysenko, quickly cut off Vavilov.

The esteemed scientist was subjected to interrogation and charged with a "systematic campaign to discredit Lysenko as a scientist," which Lavrenty Beria, the minister of the interior and head of the Communist Secret Police (the NKVD), termed a crime against the state. Lysenko set out to dismantle Vavilov's institute, including closing down the institute's publishing house and preventing Vavilov's works from being published.

In 1939 Joseph Stalin granted Vavilov a meeting. After minutes of sitting at his desk in silence, Stalin asked, "Well, citizen Vavilov, how long are you going to go on fooling with flowers and other nonsense? When will you start raising crop yields?"

Although Vavilov explained his research and the importance of the seed collection, Stalin was unmoved. Lysenko continued denouncing his opponent to the KGB (the Soviet State Security Committee), accusing Vavilov of scientific sabotage and malicious disagreement with him. Vavilov was arrested on August 6, 1940, on a botanical expedition in the Ukraine. Over the

VAVILOV'S CENTERS OF ORIGIN OF CULTIVATED PLANTS

Asia — coconut, rice, sugarcane

China — Chinese cabbage, soybean

India — cucumber, eggplant, pigeon pea

Turkey/Iran — wheat, barley, oat, fig, pea, vetch

Mediterranean — almond, cabbage, olive

Mexico/Central America — maize, tomato, cocoa, papaya, zinnia, morning glory, gourd species, upland cotton

Andes/Brazil/Paraguay — pepper, potato, rubber

Vavilov's collecting routes.

course of his imprisonment he was interrogated at least four hundred times, totaling more than 1,700 hours. Each night, Vavilov was taken from his cell and forced to stand during his ten-hour interrogations. His case went to trial on July 9, 1941, and after being found guilty, he was sentenced to death by a firing squad, but his sentence was replaced with twenty years in a prison camp. It was carried out in Saratov, where his wife and child lived, but no one told them he was there. As the Nazis gained momentum, food was in short supply and soldiers received it before prisoners. Although he was facing starvation, Vavilov never asked for his conditions to be improved, only for the opportunity to work as a teacher or a simple agronomist. Although Britain's Royal Society attempted to learn his fate and help him, Vavilov was kept hidden from anyone who could help free him. The heads of all his departments at the institute had also been arrested. None of them survived.

Vavilov was the founding father of seed collecting, but the man who spent his life focused on feeding the world died in a prison camp of starvation. He was a man of science during a time when science did not mix with the politics of Russia's ruler, Stalin.

21

CHAPTER THREE

SPOILS OF WAR

Nikolai Vavilov was not only a pioneer in seed collecting, but he also recognized how important his global collection was to his country and to the rest of the world. Unfortunately, Adolf Hitler also recognized its importance during World War II for his future Germany.

THE WORLD'S FIRST SEED BANK

The Vavilov Research Institute of Plant Industry in Leningrad, Russia, the city now known as Saint Petersburg, was home to the world's first and largest seed bank by the beginning of World War II. It housed a collection of seeds from wild and cultivated plant varieties for study and safety inside a majestic palace on Bolshaya Morskaya Street, in the heart of the city in Saint Isaac's Square. Outside the city, the Pavlovsk Experimental Station housed greenhouses and test gardens for the institute. Other stations were distributed around Russia.

The institute's scientists, led by the visionary Nikolai Vavilov, had been collecting and testing old, hardy varieties of seeds for decades from all over the world. By the time Hitler's German troops moved to strike Leningrad in September of 1941, the seed bank held seeds, known by scientists as "accessions," from 187,000 crop varieties, including crucial staple crops of wheat, corn, rice, beans, and potatoes.

23

Blue emmer Ethiopian wheat.

These metal shelves contain thousands of stored seeds.

Before the Germans advanced on the city, cutting it off from the rest of Russia, Josef Stalin, Russia's leader, ordered the art treasures in the Hermitage, just steps away from the seed bank, evacuated for their protection. Paintings were removed from frames, rolled up, and squirreled away. But there were no such plans for the small treasures gathered from five continents in the seed bank. The seed scientists were on their own. Little did they know how much Hitler also desired their collection.

Without the support of Russia's leader, the scientists risked their lives to smuggle duplicate material from the collection through the Nazi lines, over a frozen lake to a storage facility in the Ural Mountains. Other samples were taken to safe locations outside Leningrad. The scientists Abraham Kameraz and Olga Voskresenskaia dug up the potato collection from the fields at Pavlovsk despite the German bullets flying around them, and transported the collection to the institute's basement in Leningrad for safekeeping.

Leningrad's power supply was destroyed. Bombings and skirmishes were continuous. People began fighting off starvation by eating rats, pets, toothpaste, and anything else that would provide them with calories. They even added sawdust to their bread.

The siege that began on September 8, 1941, lasted for nine hundred days as the Red Army held off the Nazis. Hundreds of thousands of Russian people died, including nearly four thousand from starvation on Christmas Day, 1941. Others ate the flesh off the corpses to stay alive. The institute lost heat as temperatures outside plummeted to –40 degrees F (–40 degrees C).

Even with all the chaos going on around them, the scientists and technicians continued to work on preserving, storing, and testing their seeds. When it became too difficult to travel from their homes to work each day, they stayed at the institute. Not one scientist attempted to eat any of the seeds at the institute, even though they were growing weak from hunger and the nourishment could have saved them from starvation.

"No one even tried" to eat the seeds, recalled institute scientist Maria Bopkova in a later interview. She remembered how difficult it had been to gather the seeds for the bank in the first place and how important they were to the people of Russia.

NIKOLAI VAVILOV ARRESTED

And where was their leader during this horrible time? Nikolai Vavilov had been arrested and put in jail while on a seed-collecting expedition in August of 1940. Under the stifling totalitarian state of Josef Stalin, Vavilov and his closest associates were imprisoned.

Another scientist said, "It was hard to wake up, it was hard to get on your feet and put on your clothes in the morning, but no, it was not hard to protect the seeds once you had your wits about you."

Some workers were killed fleeing the facility. Another fifteen to twenty technicians and scientists, including Bopkova, eventually locked themselves behind the huge wooden door of 44 Bolshaya Morskaya Street to protect the valuable collection that would be needed after the war. They tried to survive on rations of 5 ounces (150 grams) of bread a day, about two slices of bread, as they stood guard and continued their work.

Every crop seed was important. They knew the seed potatoes, for example, would need to be planted to feed the people after the siege ended, but the potatoes were in danger of being frozen during the bitter winter and plundered by the starving Russians and rats.

In January 1942, groundnut scientist Alexander Shchukin died of starvation at his desk while holding a packet of peanuts. Other deaths followed, including the head of the rice collection, Dmitri Ivanov. After Ivanov's death the scientists found that he had been protecting several thousand packs of rice. That rice could have saved him from starvation, but he knew how valuable it was to Russia's people. He put their future in front of his. Liliya Rodina, the custodian of the oat collection, also died, as did Abraham Kameraz and Olga Voskresenskaia, who had saved the potatoes.

The siege continued through 1944. At the institute today, photos of the fallen scientists memorialize the lives they sacrificed so that the majority of the seed collection could be preserved for future generations.

Those seeds have since traveled the world. Legume seeds that Vavilov himself collected from Ethiopia and that were saved during the siege were shared with the Ethiopian people years later when their precious staple crop had been wiped out by drought. In fact, many of the crops that feed the world today are the result of cross-breeding with the very seeds the scientists saved during those horrific nine hundred days.

Vavilov's face carved into a stone plaque on the seed vault building in St. Petersburg.

VAVILOV SEEDS BECOME SPOILS OF WAR

THE GERMANS KNEW THE VALUE of the seeds stored in the Vavilov Research Institute when they attacked Russia during World War II. Hitler had established a special tactical unit of his paramilitary organization, Schutzstaffel (SS), to gain control of the seed bank for the Third Reich: the Russland-Sammelcommando. The Nazis looked at the seed collection as a means of making Germany self-sufficient. Their agenda for the Russian seeds included developing hybrids that would grow in colder climates and higher elevations by cross-breeding Vavilov's Russian plants and seeds with European varieties. Even before the invasion on Leningrad, German scientists from the Kaiser Wilhelm Institutes developed plans to sack the Russian research stations. As troops moved across Russia, German botanists were not far behind. The scientists and technicians were able to protect Vavilov's main collection at the institute, but by 1943 German scientists had taken control of about two hundred field stations throughout Russia and the Ukraine.

What happened to the forty thousand samples lost from those field stations remains a mystery. That theft became one of the world's greatest acts of biopiracy. All we know is that some samples were delivered to Germany and some were stashed in a secluded Austrian castle.

Both of these buildings in St. Isaac's Square house the Vavilov Research Institute.

SEED WARRIOR: DR. SANAA ABDUL WAHAB EL SHEIKH, IRAQ

If you glanced across the landscape toward the building that houses the Iraq National Seed Bank, you might not even notice it. Its sandy-colored walls and surrounding soil camouflage it well in the Baghdad desert, but not well enough to protect it from unwanted looters in the last decade. What do looters want with seeds? Although the seeds might prove to be more valuable than diamonds, they aren't after the seeds. They want the bottles they're stored in to make bombs. They want the equipment and shelving.

Iraq has an ancient association with agriculture. It is located in an area known as the fertile crescent of Mesopotamia, where man first cultivated wheat between eight thousand and thirteen thousand years ago. Thousands of species of wheat thrived there. Many of these ancient seeds were resistant to extreme heat and drought, traits very important to food crops as our climate continues to change. This makes Iraq's seed bank very important, not only to the people of Iraq, but also to the global community.

Iraq's turbulent past has threatened the seed bank more than once. As the U.S. military invaded in 2003, Iraq fell into chaos. The seeds were in terrible danger from looters. Dr. Sanaa Abdul Wahab El Sheikh, one of Iraq's seed bank scientists, worried about the seeds in the Iraqi vault as if they were "her daughters." These ancient seeds are like dinosaurs—once they're extinct, they're gone for good.

Dr. El Sheikh scrambled to fill sealed bags with the vault's irreplaceable seeds. She buried the seeds in her office garden and covered them with grass and plants. She took the most important seeds home in jars to store in her refrigerator.

Dr. El Sheikh.

Power outages and fuel shortages became common. Forced to stay home that April, Dr. El Sheikh grew increasingly concerned about the seed bank and the seeds she had buried. When would it all end? When could she go back and uncover the seeds?

After over a month, the day finally arrived. She hurried to the bank. To her horror she found that looters had stripped the building of everything that was left. But how were her seeds?

"I cried so much when I saw what they had done," she said. "The first thing I did was rush to check that the accessions were still safely buried in the garden."

The seeds were there! Dr. El Sheikh had saved them! All of the seeds would have been lost if it hadn't been for her quick thinking. Those seeds can restore Iraq's agriculture after wars have ravaged the land.

"The job of saving seeds is an important service to humanity. I keep it in spite of all the difficult challenges in Iraq. Every country has the responsibility to preserve their genetic resource. The seeds represent the legacy of truth and environment and carry with them the identity and sovereignty of their country," said Dr. El Sheikh. All the work on their behalf begins, she said, "with love and great care."

CULTIVAR VS. VARIETY

A variety of a species occurs naturally. A cultivar, or cultivated variety, has been propagated by humans. The term "cultivated" stems from a Latin word meaning "to till." Most food crops are cultivars.

Dr. El Sheikh has been working hard since then to build up the seed bank's collection. In December 2013, she was thrilled to collect seeds from a historic cultivar of rice in southern Iraq.

She gave the bag holding the seeds a kiss and said, "I adore the old cultivated rice in Iraq. I have forty-three accessions [seed collections] at the Iraqi gene bank; I found one very old, regenerated in 2013." It is always a thrill to find any variety that has been lost or was previously unknown, as in the case of this rice. These new seeds are just one more deposit she can make to increase the country's collection.

THIRSTY RICE

According to the United Nations, farmers require at least 538 gallons (2,000 liters) of water to produce 2.2 pounds (1 kilogram) of rice. This makes rice one of the thirstiest crops in the world.

THE BLACK BOX

The Vavilov scientists and Dr. El Sheikh were not the last to protect seeds in a seed bank. There are 1,400 seed banks, or vaults, across the world, but many already have been lost in military conflicts. War and agriculture don't mix. Farmers are forced off their lands, seed banks are ravaged, and scientists are often sent into exile or killed.

We hear about officials searching for a black box after a plane crash. The black box holds information that helps officials investigate the cause of the crash. Well, Iraq has its own "black box." Like other black boxes, it also holds information. This box holds genetic information in the form of Iraq's seed heritage.

When the Taliban took control of Iraq in 1996, scientists feared for the national seed bank at Abu Ghraib. Iraq's scientists had seen Afghanistan's seed bank fall in Kabul just four years earlier.

The scientists, including Dr. El Sheikh, wanted to make sure that didn't happen to the Abu Ghraib seed collection. In 1996, they packed up varieties of ancient wheat seeds, chickpeas, lentils, and fruit seeds in a simple taped-up cardboard box. The box contained seed samples but did not include the genetic identity of the seeds. For national security, the physical sample was delivered, but without the genetic information. That "black box" of seeds was then smuggled out of Iraq to the International Center for Agriculture Research in the Dry Areas (ICARDA) in Aleppo, Syria. At least these seeds would be safe.

GENETICALLY ENGINEERED (GE) OR GENETICALLY MODIFIED (GM)

Both terms describe artificially created varieties formed by scientifically altering the genetic makeup of the variety.

The scientists knew that no matter what happened in Iraq they had a small emergency stash of native seeds that could be used to restart the country's agriculture if needed. ICARDA kept them safe for several years, until Syria began to have their own military struggles. As fighting intensified, it became time for scientists at ICARDA to flee Aleppo for someplace safer. The facility in Aleppo was soon looted. The ICARDA farm in Aleppo is currently occupied by rebels, known as the Syrian Free Army. Although Internet connection and transportation are unreliable, some scientists have remained, and requests for seeds are still being processed at the center.

So where is the black box now? It's tucked away in a refrigerated vault in Jordan. Let's hope the scientists and their seeds can return to their native lands soon.

CORN SEED SPY RING

THE CORN CAPER BEGAN TWO years before the arrest, when a man was found on his hands and knees in an Iowa cornfield owned by seed producer DuPont Pioneer. The corn in question was not your average seed corn; it was a field of an "inbred" line of corn. Inbred lines are the parents of a hybrid corn. It's not sold as seed, but is instead kept by the farmer to be used for controlled breeding, and it's very valuable. It's similar to a dog breeder keeping the parent dogs and only selling the puppies.

The man took off when he was spotted, but not before the field manager noticed his license plate number. The culprit was discovered to be Mo Hailong, who claimed to be an employee of the University of Iowa, but actually worked for the Chinese seed company Kings Nower Seed. The FBI trailed Hailong as he traveled throughout the Midwest stealing seeds with a partner in a rental car. Hailong and five other Chinese nationals were arrested for conspiracy to steal trade secrets.

The FBI discovered that the group had even bought their own testing field in the United States. Some members of the group attempted to smuggle the seeds out of the United States in 2012 in Orville Redenbacher popcorn boxes and Subway napkins. The FBI is still on the case investigating additional people involved with the plot.

In the second case, Weiqiang Zhang and Wengui Yan, Chinese employees of Ventria Bioscience, were charged with stealing controversial samples of genetically engineered rice and passing them on to scientists visiting from China. Customs agents found the seeds in the delegations' luggage. If convicted the two could face up to ten years in federal prison and a fine of up to $250,000 each.

So what made them risk so much to steal these seeds? China is a major corn importer. These seeds, which companies have spent millions producing, could have played a role in boosting crop yields in China. The seeds might be small, but the ramifications for their theft could be huge. And the punishment for their theft is pretty big.

CHAPTER FOUR

VARIETY IS THE SPICE OF LIFE

A single crop fails and within a few short years more than a million people are dead. Sound far-fetched? It happened. The crop was potato. The country was Ireland.

THE GREAT HUNGER

How can the loss of one crop be so far-reaching? The Lumper potato was the staple food of the Irish people. All farmers grew it. The potatoes were rich in protein, carbohydrates, minerals, and vitamins. The people of Ireland were accustomed to the yearly "summer hunger" when there were no potatoes, but were completely unprepared for the blight that destroyed the crop in the mid-1800s. This became known as the Potato Famine, or the Great Hunger.

Without warning, a fungus traveled in the cargo of ships from North America to Belgium in the summer of 1845. Its minuscule spores drifted on the wind to the fields of Flanders, Normandy, Holland, and southern England. In just weeks they reached the Irish Lumper potatoes. The potatoes were not resistant to this invisible menace. Leaves on the plants turned black, withered, and rotted. The blight (*Phytophthora infestans*) spread as the fungus spores multiplied and blew from plant to plant. Ireland's cool, moist

34

IRELAND.—PEASANTRY SEIZING THE POTATO CROP OF AN EVICTED TENANT, IN KERRY.

summer of 1845 supplied the perfect conditions for the blight. Soon there were no potatoes to harvest, and when diseased potatoes were used to grow the next crop, it failed as well.

Potatoes are grown vegetatively, meaning that a portion of the potato is replanted. The section that is replanted is called a seed potato. Unfortunately, the potato's diseases are carried over through the seed potatoes to the new potato plants that grow. This happened in Ireland.

Food shortages occurred. Prices soared. It wasn't long before people became malnourished. Diseases spread and deaths became commonplace.

The newspapers reported people dropping from starvation in the streets daily. On December 4, 1846, the *Cork Examiner* reported the deaths of four individuals found drowned in a dyke. Upon investigation of the gruesome scene, the people were discovered to be a young mother and her three children, dressed in mud-soaked rags, their bodies frozen and partially eaten by rats. They "were in a state of hunger bordering on starvation, but how the bodies came into the dyke of water, whether by accident or design on the part of the mother, we have no evidence to show." One heartbreaking story after another filled the papers.

MONOCULTURE
The cultivation of a single crop.

During the next six years, a million people died of famine. A million more moved to other countries.

A single crop without genetic diversity; a million lives lost.

We saw how important the seed potatoes were to the Russian scientists who protected them during the Leningrad siege. The International Treaty on Plant Genetic Resources for Food and Agriculture classifies potatoes as a priority crop. As a priority crop, potatoes are judged to be one of the most important crops for food security in the world. Potatoes are considered the most important noncereal crop in the world and are grown in more than 125 countries.

The Great Hunger in Ireland teaches us that crop diversity is crucial to our survival. If more than one variety of potato had been grown in Ireland, instead of the monoculture practice of planting only a single, genetically identical variety, some potatoes might have been resistant to the lethal blight. This might have spared Ireland from such a catastrophe.

FOOD FOR THOUGHT: ANDEAN POTATOES

More than a billion people eat potatoes. I'm munching on a bag of Peru's Andean native potato chips by a company called Viva La Papa ("Long Live the Potato")! The chips, with purple or red centers, look very different from the usual ones I buy. In contrast to Ireland's agriculture at the time of the famine, Peruvian gardens in South America, the size of small backyards, still sometimes boast thirty species of potatoes. Of the five thousand potato varieties in the world, the farmers in the Andes cultivate around

A selection of South American seed potatoes.

three thousand. They range in color, size, taste, and shape. There are white, yellow, and purple potatoes. The yellow camote, known to us as a sweet potato, can be found painted on ancient Peruvian ceramics, proof that it has played a part in Peru's culture for at least two thousand years. All of these potato varieties are resistant to different diseases and thrive in different conditions. If one fails, most likely others will survive. That is food security.

BIODIVERSITY EQUALS SECURITY

Agricultural biodiversity, the variation of species within the agriculture community, is needed for our health, resources, food, and safety. It doesn't just include the variety of crop species; it also includes all organisms in the agroecosystem. That consists of the animals, microorganisms, plants, and even the bees that pollinate the crops.

Besides security, isn't variety the spice of life? Imagine eating only processed American cheese. Wouldn't we miss the cheddar, Swiss, Gouda, and Brie on our cheese plate? Or imagine having only one ice cream flavor. Wouldn't you miss all of those yummy options? They make things interesting and delicious!

The truth is that we are losing diversity on Earth at a depressing rate. According to the International Finance Corporation, one crop seed goes extinct every single day due to a variety of reasons, including disease and climate change. And each time we lose a variety, whether wild or cultivated, we lose options for the future. No wonder the United Nations declared 2010–20 the Decade of Biodiversity.

Some crops, like corn, have historic, ancient varieties that have survived for thousands of years. Corn, called maize outside the

Red maize.

United States, Australia, and Canada, was first cultivated in Mexico. Corn is packed with carbohydrates, protein, iron, vitamin B, and minerals. Although Mexico is the center of origin for maize, it is now grown in over 160 countries and is the most widely grown crop in the world. But Mexico remains one of the top producers, ranking number four in the world, and boasts many varieties.

"The corn on Mexican or Guatemalan hillsides that may seem a sorry plant to the visitor from the United States, is likely to be very properly suited to the native diet and the local soils and weather," wrote the American geographer Carl Sauer in 1952.

Sauer recognized that "a single native village may maintain more kinds of maize than the Corn Belt ever heard of, each having a special and proper place in the household and the field economy."

The word "maize" translates to "life giver" in Spanish, and it certainly is. In the ancient Mayans' sacred text, the gods are said to have created people out of cornmeal. Although these early Mexi-

cans were known as the people of corn, contemporary Mexicans also rely on this ancient grain. Unlike many other countries, such as ours, where most of the corn is grown to feed livestock and to produce ethanol fuel, Mexican corn is primarily grown to eat. There are more than nine thousand corn mills and over thirty thousand tortilla shops in the country.

Even though there are about 1,483 acres (600,000 hectares) of maize grown in Oaxaca, Mexico, producing 500,000 tons (454,000 metric tons) of grain, this amount is 100,000 to 200,000 tons (91,000 to 181,000 metric tons) short of what the people require to eat. The people of Mexico are feeling this shortage.

The U.S. Department of Agriculture points to drought as the major cause of the 13 percent decrease during the 2011–2012 growing season in the United States. Mexico has also experienced this drought.

Estella Morales pulls an ear of corn off a stalk from her field in the mountains of Oaxaca. "This corn comes from the same corn that my ancestors . . . my great-grandparents used," she says. Estella Morales and other farmers worry about the future of their corn. She uses it to make tortillas, a staple food in her country. "Sin maiz, no hay pais" is a common Mexican phrase that means "without corn, there is no country." These rural farmers strive to maintain their historic methods of growing, but the pressure of scientific technology in the form of genetically engineered crops, bad weather caused by climate change, and large corporations threaten the survival of their ancient varieties.

CORN BELT

A region in the American Midwest that is excellent for growing corn and raising livestock. It includes the states of Illinois, Iowa, and Indiana.

41

We saw how devastating the loss of a crop could be, but did you know that American corn suffered from its own blight in 1970?

Even though scientists in the Philippines warned U.S. scientists of the disease that became known as the Southern Corn Leaf Blight in 1961, farmers weren't concerned. Not long after that, the disease made its way to Mexico. The first indication of the blight in the States arrived in some fields in Illinois and Iowa in the summer of 1968. The media pretty much ignored it. After all, Americans were preoccupied with the Vietnam War and the assassinations of Martin Luther King Jr. and Robert Kennedy. The growing industry hoped that the blight would die off in the winter without the crops feeling a loss.

But it didn't. In 1969 the blight began showing up in Iowa again, and then Indiana. Ears were found to be rotten inside their husks, and stalks drooped to the ground. By 1970 the blight had taken hold of the corn crop in Florida. Still, in August of that year the news was buried beside an ad for typewriters in a short two-paragraph article on the *Palm Beach Post* business page, with the headline "Corn Blight Spreads North, South." The article reported that it was still "too early to estimate the potential damage to the nation's $5 billion corn crop."

Corn production numbers decreased across the southern Corn Belt in the United States considerably that year as the disease spread to other states, and scientists pointed again to a lack of diversity as a contributing culprit.

"In some respects, pests and diseases are as unpredictable as weather. In industrialized agriculture, genetic diversity within a crop is unlikely to provide much protection against the vagaries of weather. But genetic diversity definitely can protect against unpredictable pests and diseases, not just in maize, and not just against

Southern Corn Blight," said biologist and agricultural blogger Jeremy Cherfas.

The immediate effects of the blight fell to the farmers, who lost valuable income, but the losses rippled across the country. There was less corn to feed the nation's cattle, poultry, and pigs. There was less corn to use in food processing and distilleries. When the blight hit, the United States was exporting about 600 million bushels each year. By 1971 the blight had appeared in Japan, Africa, Latin America, and the Philippines. The threat of spreading the blight to other countries hung over the industry. The losses in the fields were far-reaching.

Our country didn't suffer the deprivation that Ireland suffered during the Great Famine, but it could have been far worse. Scien-

Non-GMO corn.

tists realized that this fungus had found a "genetic window" into the corn. In 1972 the National Academy of Sciences added its two cents. Its study *Genetic Vulnerability of Major Crops* revealed that other American crops were "impressively uniform genetically and impressively vulnerable," just like corn. Without diversity, diseases can wreak havoc on our food supply.

There are many other priority crops besides corn and potatoes. Wheat, sunflower, strawberry, rice, apple, and banana are just a few. Each of these crops faces its own challenges and threats. But, even with those threats, you probably won't find a poster featuring an endangered potato to hang on your wall anytime soon.

Conservationists know what species can get our attention. The world cares when polar bear cubs are threatened by global warming, as they should. But crops just don't have the same cuteness factor.

The U.S. Fish and Wildlife Service maintains a list of all endangered species of birds, insects, fish, reptiles, mammals, crustaceans, flowers, native grasses, and trees throughout the nation. Even though there are threatened and endangered crops, you won't find them on the list, not even below endangered toads.

U.S. corn exports grew from 600 million bushels at the time of the blight to 1,608 million bushels of corn in 2010, being shipped to such countries as Japan, South Korea, Egypt, and even Cuba. Corn is not only used for feed; it is also used to make products like glue, windshield wiper fluid, and medicines, and it is used in foods like soda, mustard, bubble gum, and ice cream. It is also processed into a biodegradable plastic.

The Global Crop Diversity Trust reported that in 1998 there were 261,584 maize seeds conserved in seed banks across the globe. How soon before we need to retrieve them?

HEIRLOOM PROFILE: GLASS GEM CORN

IS IT REAL? THAT'S WHAT most people ask when they see an ear of Glass Gem corn. The opalescent kernels of lavenders, greens, pinks, and blues shine like rare jewels. Yes, it is real. It's an heirloom variety of popcorn or flint corn. And like all heirlooms it has its own story.

The story begins with a man named Carl Barnes, a part-Cherokee farmer who grew up in Oklahoma. He spent his childhood just a half mile from where he lives now. His family was one of few that stayed on the homestead during the difficult Dust Bowl years of the 1930s. As a boy he explored his Cherokee roots and traditions. With his grandfather, he learned about the ceremonies that involved planting, harvesting, and honoring seeds. Later he was able to reintroduce many maize varieties to Native tribes. He became known as Carl White Eagle Barnes, Cherokee Corn Elder.

In this Native role, Carl shared the Native spirituality of the corn with those he met.

He saved seeds from many native and ancient maize varieties. Replanting ones that produced vibrant, translucent kernels eventually led to the creation of the beautiful rainbow variety that became Glass Gem corn.

When he reached old age he passed his seed collection on to Greg Schoen, who photographed an ear and named it Glass Gem. The name stuck. Greg passed on several varieties to Bill McDorman, the owner of an organization called Seeds Trust. Bill was amazed at what he saw, and that amazement has spread to everyone who pulls back the husk from an ear and sees the magic within.

Every ear is different. One might produce kernels in shades of lavender, while another might look like an ear of pink and red jellybeans, and yet a third might glow with yellow kernels striped with red, looking like coquina seashells on a Florida beach.

Glass Gem might have come from Carl's crossings of Pawnee miniature corns with Osage varieties, or you can believe as Carl does that it came from "Spirit."

BANANA CRISIS

Let's take a look at another priority crop—bananas. Rich in carbohydrates and minerals, such as potassium and vitamin A, bananas are found in markets and lunch boxes from London to Los Angeles, Berlin to Beijing. But in all of those places, you see mostly one variety: the Cavendish. The Cavendish banana is easy to grow and affordable, and outside of the occasional bump or bruise, it comes out of the crates looking perfect. The Cavendish is a successful crop for the banana industry. But it wasn't always the Cavendish that graced our grocery shelves.

HEIRLOOM
An open-pollinated variety that has been around for about fifty or more years and is shared within a community or family.

Ripe bananas being prepared for market in 1948.

A few generations ago, growers considered the Cavendish inferior to the tastier Gros Michel banana. The Cavendish wasn't sold anywhere until a fungus, called Panama disease, invaded banana plantations. The fungus killed off all of the Gros Michel bananas.

By the time your grandparents were taking bananas out of their lunch boxes in the 1960s, the Gros Michel was virtually extinct. What replaced it was the Cavendish, a Chinese variety that was smaller, bruised easier, and wasn't as tasty. But the Cavendish had one thing going for it that the Gros Michel didn't. It was resistant to Panama disease. And so, we've been eating Cavendishes ever since.

While we've been peeling back our Cavendish bananas these last fifty years, the Panama virus has changed and grown stronger, and it has begun to spread. It's predicted that it will reach the Cavendish banana crops in Latin America in five to twenty years. Are we prepared? The Cavendish is not immune to this new, more powerful fungus.

OPEN POLLINATION

Pollination that occurs by an insect, bird, wind, or other natural mechanism, leading to a very diverse community of plants.

47

Cocoa production dominated the islands of Trinidad and Tobago between 1866 and 1920. Here workers sort out beans on a plantation.

There are, of course, other banana species. The Yunnan wild pink banana is one of them, but it faces problems as well. A native to China, the Yunnan is threatened with extinction due to deforestation. It was the 24,200th species to be banked for safety at the Millennium Seed Bank in England in 2009. This wild relative of our cultivated banana is resistant to many common banana diseases. Perhaps its seeds might enable us to breed a new banana variety in the future.

Scientists and farmers are also looking to the Goldfinger, another banana variety growing in popularity in Australia, as a replacement for the Cavendish. Will it be resistant to the Panama virus?

If banana companies don't find a cure for the fungus or a banana that can resist it, we may have to do without banana splits or slices in our cereal bowls.

But the story of bananas is complex. Bananas and plantains are grown in over 130 countries across the globe. Many countries, including the United States, have a lot more than banana splits

GMO BANANAS AND BIOPIRACY

The Gates Foundation's investment in developing a GMO "super banana" is in question because the genes used are claimed to be the property of the Queensland Department of Industries. They come from a vitamin-rich red banana (Asupina) that was depicted in two of Paul Gauguin's 1891 paintings and are a traditional food across the Asia-Pacific region. Questions of biopiracy have been raised in using genes owned by an indigenous people that have cultivated the fruit.

to worry about. East Africans rely on bananas as a staple food. In fact, it is reported that each person in that region eats an average of 882 pounds (400 kilograms) of bananas per year — almost nine hundred pounds each!

Bananas are cheap, digestible, and nutritious, especially for children. In countries with high child mortality, bananas are important sources of nutrition. What would these children's diet be like if their countries lost that crop? Sounds like it could be as devastating as what happened in Ireland, doesn't it?

FOOD FOR THOUGHT — CHOCOLATE

C hocolate may not be listed officially as an international priority crop, but to most of us who like to nibble on our candy bars, it tops our list. According to the California Academy of Science, Americans consume an average of 12 pounds (5 kilograms) of chocolate per person per year. That's about 128 candy bars per person per year! If you think that's a lot, the Swiss double that amount!

PATHOGEN

Virus, bacterium, or fungus that causes disease.

Whether you prefer dark or milk chocolate, it all comes from the pods of cacao trees. You might think you just spotted a typo, but our sweet chocolate comes from a cacao tree, not a cocoa tree! The moisture-loving cacao trees reside in the understory of tropical rainforests. The understory is between the forest floor and the rainforest canopy. Very little sunlight reaches this layer. The crops of Criollo cacao trees (*Theobroma cacao*), first domesticated by Mayans three thousand years ago in Central America, have been forced out of the Americas by witch's broom disease and frosty pod disease to farmers in Africa. About 70 percent of the world's chocolate now comes from rainforests in West Africa. These trees are not resistant to the fungal pathogens, whose spores travel on the wind. Scientists fear that

Early workers sorting cocoa beans in Trinidad.

even with a few infected pods, we could lose a third of the world's cacao supply.

That's pretty scary, but not as scary as the belief that the fungal blight that forced the crop out of the Americas in 1989 might have been spread by agroterrorism. Agroterrorism is the use of harmful biological agents to deliberately damage crops and/or livestock. Motives might be corporate gain, a political agenda, or revenge. Think of the danger that could happen if an unwanted pest is introduced that wipes out a country's staple crop. The first introduction of the fungal cacao disease occurred near a road and the second near a river, from which it spread through plantations. It was thought to have been spread to undermine the traditional elites of the region and subvert their power. No matter what the motive, the results are far-reaching.

One way to protect the future of our cocoa supply is for agro-scientists to identify cacao trees that are resistant to diseases, artificially pollinate them, and hope their offspring will also be disease resistant. It's a slow process. Thankfully scientists in 2010 sequenced the Criollo cacao tree genome, a first step in finding a solution to this crisis. While scientists work on producing disease-resistant trees, farmers in Africa have strict quarantines to protect their crop.

Addressing climate change will also improve the safety of the chocolate supply. The rising temperature impacts the water supply needed for a healthy crop.

In the meantime, you can help by buying Fair Trade products, such as chocolate, to help sustainable cacao farms and by cutting down on the amount of energy you use.

HEIRLOOM PROFILE: RAINBOW CARROTS

WHEN I WAS A BABY my mother noticed that the color of my skin had turned a weird color and took me to the doctor. It turned out I had been eating lots of carrots; so many carrots that my skin had taken on a shade of orange. I was as orange as a carrot!

Have you ever seen a carrot any other color but orange? Even Crayola has an orange crayon named after a carrot, Neon Carrot. And yet, all carrots aren't orange.

Though it sounds like something out of a fairy tale, once upon a time carrots came in a variety of colors; purple, yellow, even white. White carrots are native to Europe, while yellow and violet are said to have originated in Afghanistan. By the 1300s cooks in Italy were using violet carrots in desserts, stewed with honey. The orange carrot we know and love evolved in the Netherlands in the sixteenth and seventeenth centuries and was brought to America. Have you ever heard of William I of Orange? It is said that the orange carrot might have been developed to honor him in leading the Dutch revolt against Spain to gain their independence.

Farmer's markets are filled with produce you won't find at the grocery store.

SEED WARRIOR: SIBELLA KRAUS, UNITED STATES

When Sibella Kraus was a young chef at Chez Panisse Café in California in the early 1980s, she had access to three species of tomatoes for her dishes: Roma, slicer, and cherry. She knew there were more, but could she entice farmers to grow them? Would they be available for her kitchen?

Those days of few options are over, thanks to her innovative idea to introduce chefs to local farmers. She decided to bring the cooks together with the growers during a special Tasting of the Summer Produce event in 1983.

On a warm August evening thirty-five chefs met forty local farmers. The farmers brought crates of melons, tomatoes, and other varieties that excited the chefs. They feasted on deep-fried squash blossoms filled with mozzarella and herbs, puff pastry tartlets with sun-dried tomatoes and grilled eggplant, and other tasty treats.

53

Questions flew between the groups about what could be grown and what the chefs would like to have. It was such a hit that the tasting became an annual event, growing each year. After seven years, there was really no need for it anymore. The connections between the farmers and the chefs had been forged. So, Kraus moved on to create the Ferry Plaza Farmer's Market in 1993, a year-round market that could supply not only chefs, but everyone, with a variety of locally grown produce, as well as regionally produced foods like cheese and wine.

Fourteen years later the word "locavore," referring to a person who eats locally produced, sustainable food, was declared the "word of the year" by the New Oxford American Dictionary.

Kraus helped launch a movement that is still growing. Farmers' markets are now nationwide and their numbers grow every year. Today professional and home chefs bring the diversity of the farm to their tables.

FARMER'S MARKETS

The bell rings and the Hudson Farmer's Market in New York's Hudson Valley is open for business. People grab their baskets and bags and head to the stands. There's everything from fresh apple strudel to heirloom red noodle beans and freshly dug rosy radishes. New York State is second to California in having the greatest number of farmer's markets in the United States. According to the United States Department of Agriculture (USDA), New York State farmer's markets ballooned from 235 in the year 2000 to 643 in 2014. There are many more markets that are probably flying under the radar. And they don't stop when the weather cools. Winter markets are also growing fast. There are now 197 listed in the USDA directory for the state of New York.

Red noodle beans and other heirlooms for sale at a farmer's market.

CHAPTER FIVE

THE NEW GENETICS

Farmers killing themselves over seeds sounds extreme, doesn't it? But that is what is happening in India: there were 270,000 suicides between 1995 and 2013. It was said that during this time an Indian farmer died every half hour. In 2011 alone, there were 14,000.

India is facing a seed catastrophe. In the last twenty years, farmers have seen a staggering loss of seed diversity, the growth of large-corporation control, and the piracy of their heritage crops. Farmers in India have become dependent on genetically modified (GM) seeds. These seeds are very different from the conventional ones they previously grew.

GENETIC MODIFICATION

Genetic modification has allowed scientists who work for large corporations to surgically reinvent the plant world. This type of breeding doesn't happen in the rock-walled gardens Gregor Mendel enjoyed when he was creating hybrid peas. Instead it happens in laboratories, with white-coated scientists and instruments that would rival the most tech-savvy chemistry labs. How is genetic modification different from the work of Gregor Mendel or Luther Burbank?

The strawberry "seeds" on the outside of each strawberry are actually the plant's ovaries.

CLASSIFICATION

All plants and animals are grouped and classified. Years ago scientists grouped everything living thing into two kingdoms—plants and animals. Today scientists have expanded the classification system. Bacteria are classified in their own kingdom, as is fungi.

The English scientist William Bateson debuted the term "genetics" in a 1905 letter as a term to describe the study of heredity. He was a huge promoter of Mendel's principles. When, decades later, James Watson and Francis Crick discovered the DNA double helix structure in 1953, the field of genetics took a giant leap forward, but no one knew where it would lead. Certainly, Watson and Crick didn't imagine their breakthrough would enter into agriculture. In the twenty years following their discovery, scientists began to modify genes to create more desirable plant species. They developed the terms "genetic engineering," "transgenesis," "genetic transformation," and "genetic manipulation," before they accepted "genetic modification" (or "GM") to describe their work.

HYBRIDIZATION VS. GENETIC MODIFICATION

Hybridization is a natural process. It occurs in nature, through cross-pollination involving two organisms. It can also occur with the help of a plant breeder, like Gregor Mendel or Luther Burbank. The resulting "cross," or offspring, receives a combination of genes from both parent plants. The two plants that have bred are compatible. A wild carrot can cross with a domesticated carrot, or two lettuces can cross with each other. We wouldn't see an eggplant and a potato crossing. And we would never see the breeding of a potato and a fish, two organisms from two different kingdom classifications!

58

THE GENE GUN

Plant cells walls are designed to resist foreign material. It's how the plant protects itself. There are two ways by which a scientist can penetrate that wall to introduce foreign DNA. The first way is to use a pathogen called *Agrobacterium tumefaciens,* which infects the plant with a gall disease. The disease, which induces a tumor in the plant, allows the foreign gene to enter the plant cell. The other tool of biotechnology scientists is a gene gun that shoots gold or tungsten particles that carry foreign DNA or RNA right into the plant cell. Scientists also call this process "biolistics." The gun can be rather inaccurate as it hits the cell, and it might create damage or not pass into the cell properly.

Genetic modification, however, occurs unnaturally, contrived by human scientists, often between two organisms that would never cross in nature. For example, Bt corn combines genes from a bacteria species and a plant, organisms from different kingdom classifications. Scientists take genetic material from the bacterium Bt (*Bacillus thuringiensis*), a microorganism that kills European corn borers, and insert it into corn to create a new variety that would never occur outside of the laboratory. The resulting variety of Bt corn is known as a GM, or genetically modified, crop or plant. Scientists also breed Bt with cotton.

Another example of a GM crop is Roundup Ready soybeans, patented by a company called Monsanto in 1996. In this case of genetic modification, soybeans are genetically engineered to grow even after being sprayed with the herbicide Roundup. The herbicide kills all the weeds around the plant, but the soybeans remain alive.

CRISIS IN INDIA

Nowadays, GM seeds are the only ones widely available to Indian farmers from local seed distributors. Monsanto, the largest seed producer in the world, came to India in 1997, bought up many small seed companies, advertised its own seed on billboards, and promised great productivity to farmers.

The genetically modified Bt cotton is attractive to farmers because it assures high yields, having been engineered to produce its own insecticide, the bacterium called *B. thuringiensis*. This bacterium protects plants against harmful bollworms. The Environmental Protection Agency classified this bacterium as a pesticide in 1968.

However, the price of Bt cotton is eight thousand times higher than the conventional seeds the Indian farmers previously bought. The high yields it promised seemed worth the elevated cost, but this cost has forced many farms into debt. Bt cotton proved to be more needy than the farmers originally thought. They believed that they would be paying a higher price, but that the genetic modification would take care of much of the needs of the crop. However, the farmers soon realized that the crop required pricey fertilizer and additional pesticides to help it grow. Even though Bt cotton emits its own insecticide against harmful bollworms, it does not protect against mealy bugs, white flies, or other pests, which can easily destroy an entire crop.

PESTICIDES
Substances that kill pests. Pesticides include herbicides and insecticides.

The costs of fertilizer and pesticides had been minimal prior to the influx of GM seeds. In the past, farmers saved their seeds from year to year and the crops needed little else. To afford these new

costs, farmers took out loans from banks and moneylenders, and used their land as collateral.

"Most Indian farmers growing Bt cotton [seeds] are either in debt or just above, because the seed cost has jumped from 7 rupes [US$0.12] to 1,700 rupes [US$28.00] a kilo. And the pesticide [price] used with these genetically [produced] Bt cotton seeds has increased thirteen-fold in four years of planting," claimed the seed activist Dr. Vandana Shiva.

The planting season in India begins with the men plowing. The women and girls join in spreading seeds. Brightly colored saris can be seen dotting the earthy landscape, as the seeds are hand-sown into the soil from dawn until dusk.

There is no irrigation in most of these farm communities. The families pray for rain, but not too much. The Bt cotton will not survive a drought, nor if it rains a lot. They pray for balance.

Fertilizers and pesticides are hand-applied to the plants, which poses health risks to the farmers doing the application. They pray for the health needed to maintain their farm.

At the end of the season, the family walks back into their fields

Farmers in India are not alone in their struggle against GM seeds. There have been protests all over the world, including the United States.

and picks the cotton that has survived. The yield is often much lower than what is expected, sometimes too low to pay back their land loans. So when the cotton crop doesn't return the investment promised by the seed distributers, the farmers are left with few options. They will try to borrow more money from a moneylender, promise their next crop to the moneylender who is holding their mortgage, or lose their land.

Some farmers have even resorted to selling one of their kid-

FOOD LABELING

Do you know if you're eating genetically modified foods? If not, write a letter to your elected officials to demand food labeling. Right now food manufacturers are not responsible for identifying genetically modified ingredients on their labels. Mandated food labeling would provide identification of all GMO ingredients so that you could make decisions about what you choose to eat.

At a march against Monsanto.

neys. Not only do they face starvation and poor health, but they also cannot pay dowries for their daughters, meaning the girls are destined to live a life without marriage and security. Children quit school to work menial jobs, and the Indian culture and economy suffer.

In the face of these horrific futures, India has seen a staggering number of distraught farmers committing suicide in the last sixteen years. It has become common for a farmer to find out he will lose his land, walk into his field, and drink the pesticide that will kill him. The children left behind, like teenager Manjusha Ambarwar, lose their fathers' protection and their childhood. Ambarwar investigates her father's death in the documentary *Bitter Seeds*.

BITTER SEEDS

Bitter Seeds, the third documentary in Micha X. Peled's Globalization Trilogy, was shot in the Vidarbha region of the state of Maharashtra in India, where there is a heavy concentration of cotton farms. The film follows a season in an Indian village from sowing to harvest.

SEED WARRIOR: DR. VANDANA SHIVA, INDIA

The Indian scientist, philosopher, and activist Dr. Vandana Shiva wants the deaths in India to stop. She also wants the control of genetically clean seeds put back into the hands of farmers all around the world.

Today Dr. Shiva is visiting Vassar College in New York State's Hudson Valley. She walks into the room dressed in a beet-red sari and sits among the students and community members. In anoth-

Dr. Vandana Shiva.

er day she'll fly to California to speak on International Women's Day, and then she'll board a flight back to New York to speak two days later at the Brooklyn Botanical Garden. Her voice is clear and commanding, despite a slight travel cough. She speaks for the seeds. She speaks for the Indian farmers. She speaks for us.

"This is not being done to improve the food supply or nutrition;

it is being done to control seed," argues Dr. Shiva about the use of genetically engineered seeds. She is a recipient of the prestigious international Right Livelihood Award.

Dr. Shiva speaks of the atrocity in India as genocide. She believes this genocide is caused by the World Trade Organization and the Indian government and that it is designed to destroy small farmers in the hopes of transforming the country's agriculture. "We call genocides the killing of five thousand people, two thousand people, two hundred people, and here is the killing of more than a quarter million," says Dr. Shiva.

She began the organization Navdanya, meaning "nine seeds," twenty-six years ago to help preserve seed diversity and help farmers save, breed, and exchange seeds. She spoke about her beginnings in the documentary film *Dirt! The Movie*, saying that she started Navdanya as her personal commitment, not knowing how many would join or how long she could continue. She also refused to obey some of the seed laws that had been imposed on farmers forbidding them to save and exchange seeds.

Dr. Shiva began with a simple idea: "A seed must be saved. A seed must be free."

As farmers in many cultures have saved seeds for centuries, farmers in India saved their conventional seeds from year to year, as well. In Hindi, the word for seed is *bija*, meaning "containment of life."

Farmers were formerly able to share their seeds and sell them. But now it is impossible to save seeds that are genetically modified and purchased from large corporations like Monsanto (and to save money by reusing the saved seeds) without risking a lawsuit for patent infringement.

"Just like we got rid of slavery, we've got to get rid of slavery of life, through patents on seeds," says Dr. Shiva.

There are many rice varieties in India. Basmati, meaning "queen of aroma," is the best known. But even this common Indian rice couldn't escape a corporate takeover. In an example of biopiracy, a Texas firm filed a patent in 1997 for native basmati rice. The firm attempted to patent the seeds, aroma, height of the plant, characteristic elongating of the rice as it cooks, and method by which it's made.

"My mother taught me how to cook rice when I was six years old," says Dr. Shiva. She and other Indians were outraged to learn that a corporation was now pirating knowledge passed from generation to generation. In 1998, Dr. Shiva's organization, Navdanya, began campaigning against the patent.

Fortunately, after worldwide complaints and protests, the U.S. Patent and Trademark Office struck out large sections of the Rice-Tec Patent No. 5663484 in 2001, in which RiceTec had claimed that it had invented the native traits of the basmati rice.

"Patents need limits and boundaries. Life forms and traditional knowledge cannot be treated as inventions," says Dr. Shiva. She continues: "Patents on our crops are a new form of biocolonialism."

Dr. Shiva sees seeds as the spinning wheels of today. She looks back at India's history. According to Shiva, as a result of the forced colonization of India by Great Britain, the people of India stopped producing cloth for themselves. Indian cotton was being taken back to England to be made into cloth. Then, she says, "It was all about getting raw material for the textile industry and

BIOPIRACY
The theft of wild or indigenous plants by corporations that then patent them for their own profit.

Dr. Vandana Shiva speaking at Vassar College.

about destroying local textiles. Gandhi said, 'We won't be free until we make our own cloth.' Gandhi taught himself and then taught everyone in India how to spin." The spinning wheels enabled the people of India to take control of their economy. If farmers are able to take control of their own seeds, they will be able to control their own agriculture.

Dr. Shiva discusses how important it is for everyone to become self-reliant. That is why she instructs others not only to grow a garden, but also to save seeds, make their own food, and grow their communities. Dr. Shiva believes that it is important to protest every law that will make self-reliance illegal.

Most, if not all, seed savers in India are women, including Navdanya's head seed keeper, Bija Devi. "When women do farming they do it for life. When women do farming they do it for their

children. They do it for nutrition. They do it for taste." She adds that corporations breed seed "for all the wrong things." She points to the fact that many of the mega-seed corporations are gaining much of their revenue from toxic chemicals, including pesticides and fertilizers. She adds that they are more interested in the money gained from long-distance commerce.

Dr. Shiva speaks from experience. Her mother left her career to be a farmer and her father was a conservator of forests. Both had a deep love of nature and instilled that love in their daughter. She tells the Vassar group about her first lesson in Gandhian economics. She was just a little girl and wanted a new, popular dress, manufactured from a fabric Indians called glass nylon, for her sixth birthday. Her mother promptly told her, "I'll get you a nylon frock, but just remember if you wear *khadi*, which is the handspun, hand-woven cloth, then a woman could light a fire and cook a meal for her child that night, and when you buy your nylon frock the rich industrialist gets his next Mercedes car. You make your choice."

"That was the end of the nylon frock," Dr. Shiva says with a smile.

When she wasn't at school, she spent most of her time in the Himalayan forests with her father. In the 1970s she and other Indian women surrounded trees to protect them from being cut down. This protest against logging became known as the Chipko movement.

She started the Research Foundation for Science, Technology and Ecology in her mother's cowshed. Dr. Shiva now speaks all over the world. India is not alone in its struggle against corporate seed patents and its fight to keep its native seeds free and pure. Before coming to Vassar College, Dr. Shiva also made a stop in

Hawaii, which has become a center of biotechnology seed experimentation.

"The earth is living. She's our mother. Our world is not for sale because the world is not a commodity," she says.

She smiles as she references Mahatma Gandhi: "Be the change you want to see."

SEEDS UNDER CONTRACT

Farmers who purchase Monsanto's patented GMO seeds must sign a contract promising not to save seeds from the crops they grow. This means that they must purchase new seeds each year.

SEED WARRIORS: DWIPEN BARUAH AND KISHOR TIWARI, INDIA

Dr. Vandana Shiva's organization Navdanya is not alone in its efforts to preserve and protect the seed heritage of India. Dwipen Baruah, a young farmer, had collected sixty local rice seed varieties from the rice paddy fields of Sivasagar and Jorhat in late 2013. Like many other local varieties, this rice is tolerant to the region's extreme weather conditions, making it very valuable.

Some call Kishor Tiwari Savior of the Dying Fields for his work to also help Indian farmers in the Vidarbha region. He's the founder of the farm advocacy group Vidarbha Jan Andolan Samiti. The fast-talking former engineer is asking for a countrywide ban on Bt cotton. He's seen its destructiveness firsthand. Tiwari has recorded cotton farmer suicides in Vidarbha—five hundred in the first six months of 2007. That number translated to three per day.

With the help of these two activists and others, there is hope for the future of Indian agriculture.

PEACEFUL COEXISTENCE?

CAN ORGANIC FARMERS COEXIST PEACEFULLY with farms growing genetically engineered seeds nearby? This battle is going on in many areas and there might not be any winners. It is taking place in farming communities throughout the United States, including Oregon's Willamette River Valley.

The valley is so perfect for growing, with rich soil and a mild climate, that settlers arriving from the Oregon Trail called it Eden. Now this planting paradise is in jeopardy. Frank Morton, an organic farmer, says, "This valley is not big enough to have genetically engineered crops and normal crops growing together without cross-contamination happening."

His concern centers on the activity of a farmer in the region who is growing vegetables using genetically modified seeds that are Roundup Ready. Morton has an organic seed business with customers in Europe, Japan, and Korea. Those customers will not buy seeds if there is a possibility the seeds contain genetically modified material through cross-pollination.

The Willamette Valley Specialty Seed Association constructed a system to avoid cross-pollination problems, but it can't prevent cross-pollination of genetically engineered seeds. In the past, local farmers came to the association's map of the valley each year and stuck a pin in it to claim an area to plant. The claims are on a first-come, first-served basis. So, for example, if one farmer pins a sugar beet field, no other farmers are allowed to grow seed for Swiss chard, which could cross-pollinate, within three miles. That's because Swiss chard and sugar beets are related in the same way a golden retriever and a poodle are—they are two different species but they're both dogs, or in the case of these vegetables, *Beta vulgaris*.

But let's say one farmer is planting organic sugar beets and another is planting Roundup Ready sugar beet seeds—now a problem exists that didn't before. GMO pollen from the Roundup Ready sugar beets, can travel miles on the wind or with the help of insects to the field of the organic sugar beets, so distance is no longer an effective barrier. The organic farmer is afraid of ending up with contaminated seeds that he cannot sell as organic if there is cross-pollination.

An issue facing farmers who grow genetically modified crops is patent infringement. In February 2013 the U.S. Supreme Court heard a case of patent infringement between an

Indiana farmer and Monsanto. It was not the first time Monsanto had squared off with a farmer in court. Monsanto had previously filed 136 lawsuits against four hundred farmers and fifty-three small farm businesses. They have won seventy of those cases, and garnered over $23 million in damages.

The case of Vernon Bowman, a seventy-five-year-old farmer, reached the highest U.S. court. Bowman claimed that Monsanto's patent does not extend to the second-generation soybean seeds he purchased at a grain elevator. Farmers are used to purchasing seeds from grain elevators that will be used for feed, milling, and other needs, but not as crop seed. Bowman had been buying the seeds and planting them for eight years.

Monsanto won the case in 2013, with the Supreme Court ruling unanimously that farmers could not use Monsanto's patented GMO soybeans to create new seeds without paying the company a fee. Bowman claimed that Monsanto is using patent law to bully farmers. Bowman had to pay Monsanto more than $84,000 in damages.

The Supreme Court, which includes Judge Clarence Thomas, a former Monsanto attorney, was not swayed by Bowman's argument.

CHAPTER SIX

A RETURN TO HEIRLOOMS

The sun has broken through the early morning fog and the crowds are already in line for the Petaluma Pie booth's savory and sweet hand pies. A young girl's voice belts out "Stand by Your Man" from an outside stage. Thousands of people have descended upon the Sonoma County Fairgrounds in northern California for the third year in a row to hear farmers, scientists, and activists from all over the world talk seeds for a week at the National Heirloom Expo.

National Heirloom Expo.

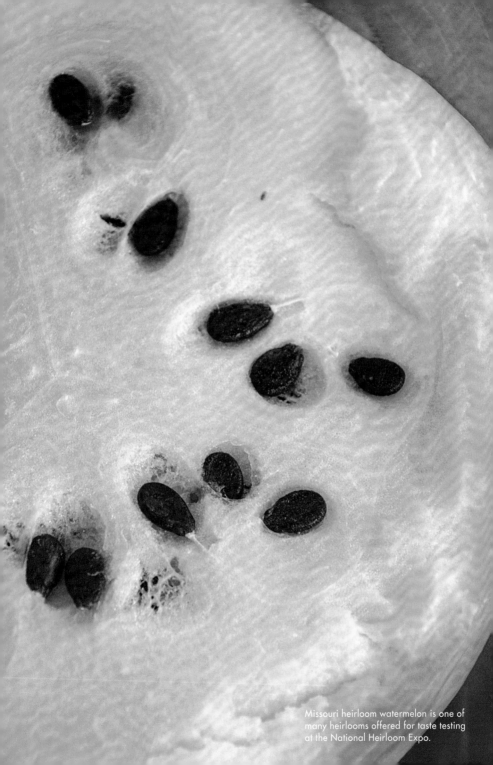

Missouri heirloom watermelon is one of many heirlooms offered for taste testing at the National Heirloom Expo.

National Heirloom Expo.

Nearby a building is filled with long tables of heirloom eggplants, squash, watermelons, peppers, and other fruits and vegetables that will rarely be found in your local grocery store. With agricultural diversity shrinking, heirloom species can provide strength and genetic variation. These distinct varieties could be historic commercial plants or heirlooms that have been grown and shared within communities and families.

LANDRACE

A local variety of domesticated plant (or animal) species that has been developed over time by its environment.

74

HEIRLOOMS STEP FORWARD

The seed collector and food historian William Woys Weaver speaks to a packed room. "Heirlooms are important in keeping the genetic diversity of our crops alive."

Weaver inherited his seed collection from his beekeeper grandfather. His grandfather allowed some of his honeybees to sting the African American folk artist Horace Pippin to relieve his arthritis in the 1940s in exchange for rare seeds, such as the fish pepper. The peppers had originally come from African American Baltimore caterers who used them to make white paprika. The fish pepper seeds are just one among the four thousand varieties of seeds that William now has in his Roughwood Seed Collection.

Weaver is credited with introducing America to heirloom varieties. In 1996 he wrote a book called *Heirloom Vegetable Gardening*. The book was the first to bring the old varieties, the heirlooms, into conversations about food and about gardening. The stories of 280 different vegetables fill his pages. Weaver even appeared on *Good Morning America* with Julia Child!

Weaver's Roughwood Seed Collection now includes fifty-five varieties of potatoes, including the large brown Irish Lumper potato that suffered from the famous blight. "That potato was originally brought to Ireland from Chile in the 1500s," he says, sharing an even earlier seed story of the famous potato.

Heirlooms ensure the survival of a species in times of stress. They have traits, sometimes hidden, that might include disease resistance or that can address the changing climate. We sometimes don't know how valuable these traits are until a crisis occurs and the traits reveal themselves.

Nikolai Vavilov wrote of plant breeding as "evolution at the will of man." Dr. Cary Fowler suggests that plant breeders create their masterpieces using the genetic variation of a crop just as artists use a broad spectrum of colors to produce a great piece of art. Heirlooms offer a multitude of variation, and if we take that variation away it's like stealing the colors from an artist. Evolution is slow to occur and extinction is more likely. Our modern plants will evolve if they are able to gain variation from breeding with their wild relatives and the ancient landraces or heirlooms. Without the genetic information from the seeds of heirlooms and wild relatives, we face a future with plants that are not hardy enough to withstand the pressures of pests and disease.

"Heirlooms are not museum foods," says Weaver. "They need to be part of our daily lives."

As a food historian, Weaver appreciates the documentation of heirlooms, which provides their historical pedigree and cultural importance. He introduces the audience to a yellow Peruvian pepper with a citrusy flavor that has been grown in Peru for two thousand years. A perfect example of a landrace, the Aji Limo de Peru pepper can be seen on pre-Columbian pottery and textiles and

Heirloom fish peppers.

has also been found in graves. Like other landraces, it was developed in a village and has been handed down as part of the culture for generations. Stories like this go hand-in-hand with heirloom seeds.

"Heirlooms are our fallback if or when everything else fails," says Weaver. "The more people who have them, the safer the seeds."

SEED WARRIOR: JERE GETTLE, FOUNDER OF BAKER CREEK SEEDS, UNITED STATES

Jere Gettle walks around a National Heirloom Expo building in overalls, a shirt, and a bow tie. He smiles next to a display of watermelons. Gettle, the owner of Baker Creek Seeds, is one of the founders of the National Heirloom Expo, which draws people from as far away as India and Australia. They come to share advice, talk about their farms, and above all, spread the story of heirloom fruits and vegetables.

Gettle speaks about a food revolution, a return to growing and eating genetically pure food. That's the reason he opened the Petaluma Seed Bank, an outlet for Baker Creek Seeds, housed in an old limestone bank building in the northern California city of Petaluma. There are fifty-five varieties of watermelon in the Baker Creek catalog; some have pink flesh, others orange, and some even have white seeds. The seeds fill several shelves at the Petaluma Seed Bank. But you might see only two or three kinds of the juicy fruits at your local store.

It's not surprising to learn that the founder of Baker Creek Seeds grew up in a gardening family. Gettle's parents and grand-

Jere Gettle.

parents all gardened. He lived in Oregon, in the Boise Valley area, and then moved to Montana when he was five. Young Jere was entranced by the odd novelty items he saw in the seed catalogs his parents used, like lemon cucumbers that have the same shape and color as sour lemons, but are actually sweeter than common cukes.

He had his very own little patch of garden when he was just three years old and remembers planting scallop squash and yellow pear tomatoes. Gettle felt that those seeds and plants connected him to faraway places, history, and stories.

Gettle started saving his seeds and by the time he was sixteen he had jars of seeds saved of many different plants. He began trading seeds through the Seed Saver Exchange, gathering even more for his collection. When he was seventeen, he began Baker Creek Heirloom Seeds and printed up 550 twelve-page sales catalogs.

Now fifteen years later, Jere Gettle's Baker Creek Seeds has not only spread to Petaluma, but he also acquired the historic Comstock Seed Company in Wethersfield, Connecticut. In addition, Gettle spreads the word of heirlooms through his magazine, *Heirloom Gardener,* and several books.

FOOD FOR THOUGHT: JOIN THE APPLE CORE!

The sweet smell of apples fills your nose even before you open the door to the orchard store. It's autumn. Apple time! Bins of golden yellow and round red apples are everywhere. Honeycrisps, Paula Reds, MacIntoshes, Empires, Macouns, and Galas crowd the shelves. There are Cortlands and Fujis. Each one sweet or tart, crisp or juicy.

In the 1800s 7,100 named apple varieties grew in the United States. That's a lot of apples! Think about that tremendous number of apple varieties, each one named by the grower. Can you imagine that many different kinds of apples in your local supermarket? You could eat a different variety of apple every day of the year for nineteen years! Regrettably, we have lost 6,800 of those varieties. Each

variety carried a specific genetic code. That code was responsible for the variety's taste, color, and resistance to diseases or blights. Each time a species becomes extinct, we lose its genetic code and our earth's biodiversity decreases.

Northern Californians are working tirelessly to save their local Gravenstein apple from oblivion, but they have two major obstacles. First, old orchards are being transformed into profitable vineyards to produce wine. And second, the apple industry competes with cheap apple juice concentrate coming from China.

The 20 square miles (32 square kilometers) of Gravenstein trees that once covered the hills in nearby Sebastopol, California, have been reduced to one mile. Thankfully, the Gravenstein is not endangered worldwide—it's still a favorite apple in northern Europe, the Pacific Northwest of the United States, and Nova Scotia, Canada—but these tall, iconic apple trees are struggling to withstand the pressure of more profitable crops after over a century of history in the Sonoma region.

Not only is the land the orchards are on more valuable to vineyard farmers, but farming the Gravensteins is a challenge. One of the few remaining Gravenstein farmers, Lee Walker, claims he loses 40 percent of the apples due to the stubby, weak stems that have trouble holding the apples in the wind.

So why save them?

Gravensteins have an intense flavor and a distinctive fruity, floral aroma. The scent is so strong that it even remains on your fingers after washing them. Because of its unique taste and aroma, the apple became so popular a century ago that it helped Sebastopol prosper. Roads, schools, and festivals were named after the Gravenstein. In fact, American soldiers serving abroad during World

War II were given Gravenstein applesauce and dried apples from those very trees in Sebastopol.

The Gravenstein, with origins in seventeenth-century Denmark, pops up in an apple pie at the National Heirloom Festival at the nearby Sonoma County Fairgrounds. The line of people at the Gravenstein pie booth indicates its popularity. Beside the glass cake stand is a pile of bumper stickers—"Save Our Gravensteins."

A group called the Apple Core is spreading the word to preserve this unique species for Northern California. The simple first step they suggest to help any of these threatened species to survive is—ask for it by name!

Kidd's Orange Red apples are a cross between Cox's Orange Pippen and Red Delicious. They were introduced in 1924.

BIJA DEVI AND NAVDANYA

Bija Devi doesn't speak much English, but that doesn't stop scientists, students, and researchers from flocking to the forty-acre farm near Dehradun, in the foothills of the Himalayas of India, that she tends with Dr. Vandana Shiva. They come to hear her speak. Devi, seed keeper for Dr. Shiva's organization Navdanya, teaches younger generations about seeds, sustainability, and seed saving.

"Before you learn anything, you should learn to respect food," says Devi.

She grows over a thousand varieties of "lost" cereals, fruits, and vegetables, and close to 1,500 varieties of rice alone.

Devi remembers when farmers would use cow dung as fertilizer for their crops instead of the chemicals that are used today. They saved seeds to cultivate on their own farms. The grasses and weeds that grew among the crops were used to feed the cows, who gave the farmer milk to drink and turn into cheese and butter. It was simple. But as we know, life on the farms has changed in India.

CEREALS

You might only think of cereals as a boxed breakfast food, but cereals are also the grains used to make the breakfast food you eat. They include wheat, rice, oats, and corn. The next time you pour yourself a bowl of Special K or Froot Loops, think about the crops that were grown in order to produce it.

Navdanya has established fifty-four community seed banks across sixteen states in India. With Devi's help the organization has provided salt-water-resistant heirloom seeds to areas recovering from cyclone damage, drought-resistant seeds in drought-damaged Bundelkhand, and flood-resistant seeds to flooded Bibar.

Dr. Shiva is addressing other problems with India's agriculture, including the biopiracy of basmati rice. The seawater that washed over the Indian landscape during the devastating 2004 tsunami left behind salt. It made farming with GM seeds impossible. Thanks to the community seed banks organized through Navdanya, Indian farmers were able to obtain the native salt-tolerant rices that grew in the coastal areas. Heritage seeds proved to be priceless and irreplaceable.

Devi works to preserve biodiversity by promoting seed saving among India's farmers.

WHY PLANT HEIRLOOMS?

Quality: Heirlooms offer a variety of tastes and, in some cases, higher nutritional content than some modern breeding varieties.

Seed saving: Heirloom seeds can be saved from year to year and will grow true to type each year. Hybrid seeds can be saved, but the resulting plants will exhibit traits from both parents and might not display the characteristics you want.

Performance: Heirlooms grown over generations are usually quite hardy, providing farmers with consistent results.

History and tradition: Heirlooms come with stories that are continued and added to by farmers who plant them. They are a legacy that is given to us from the past and that we give to the future.

CHAPTER SEVEN

THE ULTIMATE SAFETY NET

You take a flight to Norway and manage to arrive on the frozen island of Spitsbergen. You're about 620 miles (998 kilometers) from the North Pole, in a land where polar bears roam free and it's illegal in some areas to travel without a gun for protection. Once there, you rent a snowmobile, dodge the polar bears, and follow the Svalbard Global Seed Vault's beacon of light to its entrance. Designed by Norwegian artist Dyveke Sanne, triangular segments of mirror, steel, and prisms are lit by a network of fiber-optic cables that reflect turquoise and white lights during the long winter.

You park your snowmobile, lift your goggles from your eyes, and look around.

Everything here is white. White snow. White sky. White mountains. So many shades of white, they start to look blue or pink. You're white-blinded.

Except for the vault, everything you see is white.

Now to get inside.

The vault is designed for high security. You need to pass through four locked doors, each with a separate key. First, you pass through the heavy steel entrance; then it's 126 yards (115 meters) down a cool tunnel.

Seeds at the Svalbard Seed Vault don't really sit on ice, but they *are* kept very cold.

85

It's quiet inside the vault, but the sounds of howling outside sometimes penetrate the tunnel. Wind. Wolves. A small shudder goes up your spine as you continue on.

Finally, you reach two air-locked, key-coded doors. Even if you had all the keys to all the doors, motion detectors would alert security to your arrival. These seeds are in serious lockdown!

DOOMSDAY VAULT

There are more than one thousand seed banks throughout the world, but this bank is different. It doesn't hold the seeds of one country. It holds duplicate seeds from any country or institution that wants to have a backup to their collection. Like a safe-deposit box in your local bank, the seeds can be accessed only by their owner. Norway, home to the Nobel Peace Prize, is trusted with the safety of these duplicate collections. It neither owns nor controls them.

And the bank is inside a mountain.

The vault was dreamed up in part by agriculturist Dr. Cary Fowler. It is Norway's gift to the world. The Norwegian government built and financed the vault. It's carved four hundred feet (122 meters) into a mountain. The Global Crop Diversity Trust, founded by the United Nations in 2004, is in charge of collecting and maintaining the seeds.

The Svalbard Global Seed Vault, nicknamed the Doomsday Vault, opened in February of 2008 with a grand ceremony. Blue light lit up the tunnel into the frozen mountain, and for the first time the sound of the wind was replaced with haunting native Norwegian music.

Cryogenic tanks at the Vavilov Institute hold samples to be sent to Svalbard.

One hundred and fifty delegates watched as the prime minister of Norway, Jens Stoltenberg, opened one of the inside doors. Then, together with the Nobel Peace Prize winner, environmentalist, and African tree planter Wangari Maathai, he placed the first treasure box of seeds into the bank. What did it contain? Varieties of rice seeds from 104 countries. The first of many deposits!

Next came 268,000 distinct samples of seeds—each one originating from a different farm or field in the world. They filled 676 boxes, weighing roughly 11 tons (10 metric tons). There were maize, rice, and wheat seeds from Asia and Africa, and eggplant, barley, and potato from South America and Europe.

The vault can store 4.5 million seed samples, which will represent every variety of the world's most important crop seeds from countries all over the world. It's like a Noah's Ark of seeds.

Someday the vault will hold "samples of five hundred seeds of every variety of agricultural crop that can be stored in a frozen state," says Fowler.

FROM RUSSIA WITH LOVE

Russia is now one of the countries sending seeds to Svalbard for safekeeping. "The shelf life of seeds at room temperature is only one to five years," says Boris Makarov, manager of the cold storage facility at the Vavilov Institute, on my visit. To maintain those seeds, scientists need to take them out of storage every two to three years and allow them to germinate and go to seed again. "Cold storage allows them to be stored many more years—decades," he adds. With Cary Fowler's help and direction, the Vavilov seeds are making their way to the Svalbard vault.

The vault's location helps maintain the cold temperatures needed to prolong the seeds' lives. The permafrost, rocky location, and refrigeration system keep the vault at 25 degrees F (–4 degrees C) or colder at all times.

"The seed vault is the perfect place for keeping seeds safe for centuries," says Fowler. "At these temperatures, seeds for important crops like wheat, barley, and peas can last for up to ten thousand years."

It is estimated that the demand for food and feed crops will almost double within the next fifty years as the rate of population increases. Nevertheless, the rate of population increase is above the estimated increase of yields for the three most important crops—wheat, maize, and rice.

Consider that the world also faces threats through natural and manmade disasters, and the vault becomes even more important. The seeds can remain in the vault safe from any disaster until each country withdraws them.

Seeds are readied at subzero temperatures for Svalbard storage.

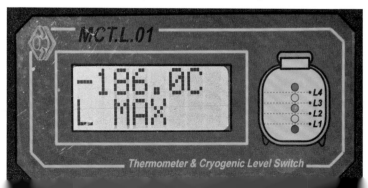

WE'RE TALKING *OLD* SEEDS

IMAGINE FINDING A SEED that is more than two thousand years old. Archaeologists uncovered ancient date palm seeds in 1973 while digging through the dirt of the storeroom at Masada, a cliff fortress built by King Herod in Israel. The seeds ended up labeled and placed in a drawer with other items.

Could these seeds ever sprout? Even though their skin had become much harder over those two thousand years, Dr. Sarah Sallon decided to give them a try. How fantastic it would be to have these seeds germinate! The Judean date palms that existed two thousand years ago have long been extinct, wiped out by the conquering Romans. Those ancient palms were a staple crop and symbolized good fortune. In fact, the name Tamar, given to King David's daughter, is the Hebrew word for the palm.

Dr. Sallon gave the seeds to Dr. Elaine Solowey, an expert on desert agriculture. When asked to germinate the seeds, Dr. Solowey doubted she could do it. After months of research she began by soaking the seeds in hot water to soften their seed coat. Then she placed them in an acid solution rich in hormones. After letting the seeds soak in a fertilizer made of seaweed and other nutrients, she finally was ready to plant them.

She chose the Jewish holiday of Tu B'Shevat, known as the New Year for Trees, as the day to plant the seeds, so on January 26, 2005, she planted them in fresh potting soil, set up an irrigation system, and held her breath. About six weeks later the soil cracked and a tiny sprout appeared. By March 18 she could see it was a date shoot. After all those years, one of the seeds had germinated.

The date palm that grew is male and produces pollen, not fruit, but scientists have several immature palms that have not flowered yet.

"We're hoping that one is female, so that we can revive the same kind of dates people ate in biblical times," says Dr. Solowey.

Imagine that!

Scientists know that seeds can be saved for a long time, and under the right conditions, might even germinate.

SEED WARRIOR: DR. CARY FOWLER, UNITED STATES AND NORWAY

I sit across from Dr. Cary Fowler, another recipient of the Right Livelihood Award. A black-and-white photo of his grandmother's Tennessee farmhouse hangs near his desk. His grandmother grew cotton, corn, soybean, and an assortment of vegetables on her farm in Madison County. Outside his office window in New York's Hudson Valley, zinnias bloom and melons ripen in the sun. Dr. Fowler never seems to be very far from seeds and gardens.

Dr. Cary Fowler.

About thirty-five years before the Svalbard vault was constructed, Dr. Fowler read an obscure article by botanist and agronomist Jack Harlan (son of Harry), who described the diversity within crops as a genetic resource. Harlan wrote about the loss of crop diversity. This genetic resource, he said, "stands between us and catastrophic starvation on a scale we cannot imagine."

After reading this, Dr. Fowler knew he had to act. He carved out his own career within the field of agriculture—a career that encompassed law, ecology, genetics, biology, and the history of agriculture, among other things. It brought him to Norway, where he became a professor and director of research in the Department for International Environment & Development Studies at the Norwegian University of Life Sciences. He was also a senior advisor to the director general of Bioversity International.

TRAPPED

Plants don't have the ability to move out of harm's way, like animals do. They don't migrate, either. Think about the plants in your house. What happens if you forget to water them? Or leave them in a sunny window too long? It's the same with crops that face drought conditions or other changes in their environment.

Dr. Fowler recognized that there was a mass extinction happening in our fields, one that few people noticed.

Our agriculture system had changed dramatically. Plant breeding gave farmers the tools that created breakthroughs in crop development. Farmers concentrated on crops that increased production to lower food costs. Dr. Fowler likens these agricultural advances to a "snake eating its tail." Agriculture was growing by leaps and bounds, but at a very high cost—the loss of crop diversity.

SEED COUNT

The number of samples grows every day. As of March 2014 the vault had 820,000 distinct varieties of food and agricultural crops represented.

If that weren't enough, recent climate changes have caused the decrease of more and more species. Pollution has also taken its toll. More than 13 million tons (12 million metric tons) of crops harvested each year in China are contaminated with heavy metals, according to the Ministry of Environmental Protection. In addition, pesticides have polluted 22 million acres (8.9 hectares) of Chinese farmland.

Our loss of plant biodiversity had been a problem, but now it is a crisis: a silent, rapidly growing crisis that threatens our own existence on the planet. Plants are going to need to adapt to climate change. "Are they ready to adapt?" asks Dr. Fowler. "We know they're not."

His idea for a vault, to function as a backup for the world's individual seed banks, wasn't always well received. It was a major undertaking that required cooperation from many countries and many scientists. Thankfully, he persisted. "You've got to try. Maybe one person will say, 'That's interesting,'" says Dr. Fowler. "That may be all the support you need." His plan became a reality after the International Treaty on Plant Genetic Resources provided a framework for conserving the world's crop diversity in 2004. Construction began on the frozen island in Norway in 2006.

"If we are going to survive as a species, it will be because we've learned to share that heritage," Dr. Fowler says. "I know this is just a cave in a mountain, but it's also the only thing I can think of that is really tangible, positive, and directed toward the future, with virtually all the countries working together. Maybe there's a lesson in that."

Dr. Fowler leans into his desk. "Instead of a finger in the dyke, we need to be more pragmatic. It's better to try to do something,"

he says. He believes we need to get our own hands dirty instead of just blaming other people and telling them what they need to do. "There are no bad people in this story," he says.

Dr. Fowler has certainly heeded his own advice. He knows that the biodiversity crisis train has left the station, and that we no longer have the luxury of not acting. "There is a saying," he says: "'The dogs bark but the caravan moves on.'" He gives a laugh. "In other words, get on with it."

The Svalbard Vault is up and running. And the world has noticed. In 2010, the Russian Academy of Agricultural Sciences awarded Dr. Fowler the Vavilov Medal for his "exceptional contribution" to the cause of conserving plant genetic resources, and this is just one of many accolades he has received for his persistence and hard work on behalf of plant genetic diversity.

I stand with Dr. Fowler in front of his orchard and he tells me that as of August 2013, the vault has accepted 783,336 samples, or 4,411 species from 231 countries and 55 institutions.

Dr. Fowler has made a difference, but he knows that all of us have the ability to help in this crisis. "I just wanted to be part of the bucket brigade. It doesn't matter who throws that last bucket on the fire; it just matters that you are part of putting it out."

SEED WARRIOR: SHEILA MURRAY, UNITED STATES

At the Arboretum in Flagstaff, Arizona, the horticulturist Sheila Murray is collecting seeds for England's Millennium Seed Bank. Like most seed collectors, she spends much of her days in the fields searching for the plants on a list. Sometimes she locates a species she needs, but finds only one or two plants growing. The

bank requires its seeds to be collected from plant populations of fifty or more plants in order to acquire the specific genotype, or genetic makeup. This requires year-round plant exploration!

Once the appropriate plant population has been located, Murray goes back every other week, watching the progression of the plants as they go to seed. When the seeds are finally ready to be collected, she heads back to the area with a group of volunteers and collects 20 percent of the available seeds. It is tedious work. The bank requires a minimum of 10,000 seeds that are capable of growing, or *viable*, from each plant species. Luckily, Murray doesn't have to count those herself. The bank checks each seed for viability and provides the count to Murray. Sometimes it's virtually impossible to collect those numbers because some plants don't produce many seeds.

The Millennium Seed Bank accepted its billionth seed in 2007 to mark International Biodiversity Day. Unlike many of the other banks, the Millennium Seed Bank specializes in safeguarding wild plant seeds. Its goal is to collect seeds, data, and specimens of twenty-four thousand plants, including the entirety of United Kingdom seed-bearing plants.

CITY SEED BANK

Blades of beach grass are sprouting up out of the sandy soil at the Greenbelt Native Plant Center in Staten Island, New York. The thirteen-acre center, run by the New York City Department of Parks and Recreation, grows native plants that are used to restore and maintain the city's natural areas. You might not think of New York City, one of the world's major urban centers, as having many natural areas, but there are ponds, meadows, salt marshes, and upland forests located throughout the city's 301 square miles.

The beach grass has already reached a height of about 8 inches (.2 meters) on this one-year anniversary of Hurricane Sandy's October 2012 landfall on the East Coast. Seed collectors Clara Holms and Heather Liljengren stop in front of the field. Sprinklers spray back and forth in the warm afternoon sunshine. What a difference a year can make.

Hurricane Sandy not only wreaked havoc with the human lives on the coast, but it destroyed the landscape as well. It left many coastal sand dunes in need of restoration. Acting as cushy sea walls, dunes protect communities from surging waves and tides that can flood homes and businesses. The webbing created underground by the roots of the grasses helps hold the sand of the dunes in place and protects the dunes from erosion caused by wind and water. The damage caused by this superstorm was significant and would have been even worse if the dunes hadn't been there in the first place. It's crucial to restore them to protect the shore from future storm damage.

That's where Holms and Liljengren come in. Seeds from the beach grasses were collected and banked in the seed bank at the plant center before the hurricane. Now the seeds have been withdrawn from the bank, germinated, and planted in a field laid with trucked-in sand. Those grasses will soon be able to help in the restoration project.

Liljengren points out that all plants grow in communities. They evolve together and there are checks and balances to keep the community healthy. "You can think of the plants in a community as friends who love to coexist together," she says, smiling.

Native plants are hardy. They have evolved to thrive in the soil in which they live and to tolerate local weather conditions. But even native plants face threats. Invasive species disrupt the community

Plant material and seeds drying on tarps.

and often push out natives. The disruption of weather patterns, caused by climate change, also threatens populations of wild plants.

We walk into one of the small buildings on the property, built near the old farmhouse that now holds the plant center's offices. Tarps laid out on the concrete floor are covered in plant material waiting to be cleaned.

The seeds that will be gathered from the plant material come from the founders' fields off the property. Those seeds might come from five different native collections that have been planted and harvested this autumn. They've been allowed to cross-pollinate, creating a strong genetic basis for the seed they will produce.

There are different ways of cleaning seeds to store. They might need to be scrubbed by hand on a small piece of black stair tread to separate the seed from the chaff. They might first be shaken manually on a screen. Or they might be placed into a clipper machine that does the shaking over a screen mechanically.

Good seeds, the seeds with an embryo inside, are heavier than seeds that have not produced an embryo or are underdeveloped. The good ones will fall through the screen, leaving the plant matter, underdeveloped seeds, and chaff behind.

CROSS-POLLINATE

To transfer pollen to one flower from another variety; its seed then is a mixture of both parents.

Seed scrubbing cleans seeds before storage.

"These native seeds give you the natural diversity, whereas most nurseries selling native plants are really selling you clones that have been grown not from seed, but from rootstock or cuttings," says Liljengren.

Holms adds, "Not only are these native seeds important for our restoration projects, like the dunes, but they also benefit our pollinators, which are needed for all our plants, including our crops."

Clipper machine at the Greenbelt Native Plant Center in Staten Island, New York.

Seeds in storage bags.

After the seeds are cleaned they are ready to be stored. "We're really putting the seeds to sleep in a cool, dry place," says Liljengren. We step into the seed bank, which looks similar to a large walk-in restaurant freezer with shelves lining the walls. The cool temperature of 59 degrees F (15 degrees C) and 15 percent relative humidity will slow the seeds' metabolic processes down. They can be stored here for fifteen to twenty years for safekeeping.

Germination trays.

But the seeds don't come out of this room and go right into the ground. The native plants are used to going through four seasons in this region, so they must go through their winter period first. The seeds are stored in the "winter room," where the temperature is kept around 41 degrees F (5 degrees C) and the humidity at 89 percent. They'll stay in there thirty, forty-five, or ninety days, depending on the species, before being planted in the propagation greenhouse to germinate.

INSIDE THE VAVILOV HERBARIUM

Dr. Tamara Smekalova, head of the Vavilov Research Institute's Agrobotany Department, sits across from me at an old wooden table in a room housing the herbarium. Cabinets from the early days of the institute fill the room. A small table holds an artificial, decorated New Year's tree. It's January and the Christmas and New Year holidays are still in the air. The herbarium is over one hundred years old. It was developed in parallel with the institute's seed collection and contains over thirty thousand precious sheets of paper. It resides in the institute's second building in Saint Isaac's Square.

Herbarium cabinets filled with specimens.

Heirloom apple specimen page at the Vavilov Herbarium.

Dr. Smekalova flips open one of the many folders that fill the herbarium cabinets. Inside is one sheet with a pressed and mounted specimen of a collected apple species. It includes a branch with leaves and flowers. Brown, shriveled slices from the apple and thin, crescent-shaped segments of the fruit's skin are affixed to the page beside the leaves. A handwritten label describes the specimen in Russian and notes the date when it was collected and the location.

"We are working for the future," says Dr. Smekalova.

Each time seeds are collected in the field, a sample of the plant is also collected. It is then pressed between old pages of Russian newspapers.

"This is very important for scientists. The herbarium collection gives us the opportunity to compare the same species, for example, or subspecies, from all the territory of its distribution."

Dr. Smekalova opens another folder and flips over the sheets. They bear Nikolai Vavilov's stamp, and one even has his actual sig-

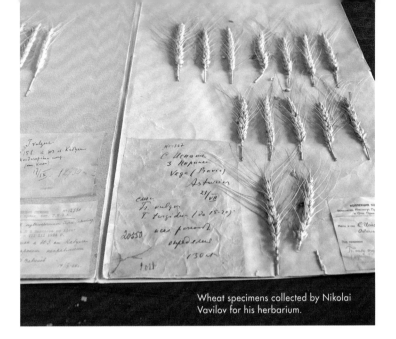

Wheat specimens collected by Nikolai Vavilov for his herbarium.

nature. These are just some of the many plants he collected on his expeditions. A sample of fragile dried wheat is still safe and sound after all these years. Since Vavilov collected samples in the 1920s and '30s, technology has changed. Scientists now have the ability to extract DNA from the herbarium samples in the event of an emergency.

The herbarium allows scientists to "see how a species in one area can change from year to year," says Dr. Smekalova. Plants are dynamic. They change over time. Their leaves might alter in shape or their flower size might change. The samples' importance in relation to the seed collection cannot be overemphasized.

Dr. Smekalova talks about her own expeditions to collect new herbarium material. Ten years ago she visited the territories in Portugal where Vavilov had visited sixty to seventy years earlier. "We couldn't find these fields, these places, because the cities appeared very quickly and destroyed all the area."

CHAPTER EIGHT

HOPE AND ACTION

D r. Cary Fowler talked about being a part of the "bucket brigade," and fortunately, he isn't the only one who has taken up a bucket during this crisis. As you've seen, there are individuals all over the world working to save, plant, and protect our seed diversity.

HOPE

I n 1980 there were twenty farmers' markets in the state of California. By 2013 that number had grown to eight hundred. Why? Because more and more people care about the food they eat, thanks to people like Michael Pollen, Barbara Kingsolver, and others who have added their voices. In 2013 there were an estimated eighteen thousand community gardens throughout the United States and Canada. Each year that number continues to grow.

In addition, seed libraries have sprung up across North America and Europe (see Resources). A seed library, usually located in a public library, "lends" out seeds to patrons. The seeds can usually be found in a set of drawers where gardeners pick out a variety and record what they have checked out. There is no cost involved, just the simple understanding that the gardener will grow the variety and bring back some of the seeds after their harvest to share with other patrons. One of the very first was the Hudson Valley Seed Library started by Ken Greene.

Eggplants and carrots
at a farmer's market.

SEED WARRIOR:
KEN GREENE, UNITED STATES

Ken Greene greets me with a smile on his face and his dog, Rutabaga, at his feet when we meet under the trees outside his office. He's got a container filled with star-shaped Hardy Hibiscus seedpods and another filled with Sulphur Cosmos seeds.

"The Cosmos are still blooming," he mentions.

We walk around the trailer to the seed gardens. The two-acre garden stretches out before us in the early-morning autumn sunshine. Already I spot rows of flowers and squash, but as we step inside the fencing the different crops come into view. It's harvest time. Many seeds have already been harvested, but rows of long Ping Tung eggplants still hang on their vines, curvy Violina Rugosa butternut squash ripen on the ground beside them, and dried Panther edamame soybean pods hang ready to be picked.

The garden is very different from the local farms you see along the loopy Hudson Valley roads and behind farm stands. With everything moving beyond the ripe stage, nothing will show up at market. These squash will not be served at your table. The lettuce

Ken Greene in front of a display of seed packet art.

overgrows to sizes you'd probably never see at the local grocery store. Everything is grown with its seeds in mind.

Like so many seed defenders, Greene has always been interested in plants. He grew up near Wellesley College, outside Boston, and when given the choice, he always suggested family outings to the college's greenhouses. He grins as he remembers planting Johnny Jump Ups in preschool.

NATURE'S WAY

Think back to those early fruits that fell and shattered to spread their seeds. Nature is designed to keep plants growing. When an overripe fruit falls to the ground and rots, the plant's seeds are resown into the earth. With many plants, like squash and eggplants, seed keepers need to let the fruits get overripe, well past the eating stage. With other plants, like lettuce, the plants need to go to seed.

"I can remember the flowers coming up each year under the crabapple tree where I planted them," he says.

Although Greene has had a lifelong love of plants, he developed the Hudson Valley Seed Library through his sense of activism. "I didn't want to be a grower; I wanted to make a difference," he says. And he has.

Stories, art, seeds, activism, and books weave through Greene's path to starting the Hudson Valley Seed Library. As a librarian at the Gardiner Public Library in New York's Hudson Valley, Greene collected vintage seed catalogs and packets. He sought out and found the stories they told. "All seeds have stories. If you lose the seeds you lose the story," says Greene. "The stories of seeds are not big, historical stories. They're personal."

Greene relishes the growing details and personal culinary stories that are shared with seeds' growers. "Growers know if what they planted is best eaten the day of harvest. Or if it is better for canning or drying. Or what recipe works best with it."

Panther edamame seeds drying at the Hudson Valley Seed Library.

. Those personal details are important to Greene. "It's a lot like oral tradition. The plants are always going to change genetically depending on the person saving the seeds and where they are. The grower is always adding to the personal story. The seeds are always evolving both culturally and horticulturally."

Greene had an idea. Libraries, long the place to share ideas and imagination, could also be a place for sharing seeds. He decided to bring seeds into his library where the local community could access them, and created the very first seed library in the nation.

We walk past a row

HEIRLOOM PROFILE: VIOLINA RUGOSA BUTTERNUT SQUASH (*CURCURBITA MOSCHATA*)

The Hudson Valley Seed Library decided to try a very rare variety of squash this year. After a time in the trial gardens, the squash made it into the seed garden. Its violin-shaped fruits have warty, apricot-colored skin. In fact, Violina Rugosa translates from Italian to "wrinkled violin." Each squash yields about 3–4 pounds (1–2 kilograms) of edible flesh that is sweet and rich, and roughly twenty-five seeds. A perfect squash to roast for Thanksgiving!

Violina Rugosa.

of shoulder-high, yellow multipetaled marigolds in the seed garden. They are quite different from the shorter varieties so common in flower borders. Greene holds a flower in his hand. "Our intern brought the seeds for these back from Mexico."

He smiles. The story continues, for these marigolds and the many other plants that are in the gardens of the Hudson Valley Seed Library.

SEED WARRIOR: DR. ELAINE SOLOWEY, ISRAEL

Dr. Elaine Solowey is working from the ground up. Without adequate soil, even heirlooms and wild plants won't succeed. Elaine works with a group at the Arava Institute's Center for Sustainable Agriculture.

While it is important for people to know how to grow something for their own consumption, she believes there is a "learned

helplessness about modern people" that scares her. They don't know how to sustain themselves with their own garden, she says.

In addition, you can't grow a garden in the Middle East without first making the soil. Plants won't grow in rocks and clay. That is where Dr. Solowey steps in.

For gardeners to grow anything at the institute, they must pile up sand, manure, and compost in raised banks called berms under Dr. Solowey's instruction. As the compost rots down, soil is created. That soil will stay alive and provide the base for a healthy garden.

Dr. Solowey teaches her students that if they can grow a garden in the harsh environment of the Middle East, then they can grow a garden anywhere. The best way to restore the fertility of the soil is by planting trees. The trees provide nuts while the soil is being replenished. The leaves of the tree fall and rot, providing more soil.

SCATTERED CORN AND JAMIE HOLDING EAGLE, UNITED STATES

Scattered Corn was the last corn priest of the Mandan tribe of North Dakota. Her role was to bless the corn seeds and distribute them to the tribe. In the spring of each year a special ceremony took place to promote the health of the corn crop. Songs were sung and the singers would sway like the corn in the wind. It was said that the singers would enter into a trance and corn would sometimes be seen coming out of their mouths.

Today, Scattered Corn's great-great-granddaughter, Jamie Holding Eagle, follows in her footsteps. After studying biology and genetics, Holding Eagle started gardening. She began the Red River Seed Library in the public library of Moorhead, Minnesota, in 2013.

ACTION

It is easy to get bombarded by all of the issues facing our earth, and we can easily get overwhelmed, but as seed activist Wangari Maathai said, we all need to be like the hummingbird. She told the story of the hummingbird in *Dirt! The Movie*.

"The story of the hummingbird is about a huge fire in the forest. All the animals in the forest come out. And they are transfixed as they watch the fire. They are overwhelmed. Very powerless. But the tiny hummingbird says, 'I'm going to do something about the fire.' So it flies to the nearest stream. It takes one drop of water and drops it on the fire. It flies back and forth, back and forth, bringing one drop at a time. Meanwhile all the animals are standing helpless. Even the big elephant, which has a big trunk, and can bring much more water. They stand helpless. They say to the hummingbird, what can you do? You are too little. The fire is too big. Your wings are too little. Your beak is too small. You can only bring a little drop. The hummingbird answers, 'I am doing the best I can.' That is what all of us should do. We should always feel like the hummingbird. What can I do, little me?"

She adds, "Even if what you are doing might be very small, might feel very insignificant, collectively if so many of us dream the same thing we would accomplish a lot."

Like the bucket brigade.

All of the seed defenders within these pages have added their buckets to the brigade, contributing their voices and their actions to help preserve biodiversity and protect our seeds from destruction.

You can, too.

CALL TO ACTION

WE CAN'T WAIT TO PROTECT OUR SEEDS. THE TIME TO ACT IS NOW. HERE'S WHAT YOU CAN DO:

❧ SAVE SEEDS

It's easy to save your own seeds. You can start with some heirloom tomatoes that you've grown yourself or have purchased at a farmer's market. There are so many varieties to choose from. Pick one that you will want to plant and eat next year. Or share with another gardener. Tomatoes are a great plant to start with because they produce a lot of seeds, typically fifty to several hundred seeds per tomato. Think of all the future tomato plants you can start!

To begin saving seeds you must start with fully ripe tomatoes. Cut them open, scoop out the pulp and seeds, and place it in a bowl to ferment for about three to five days. Add water to the pulp

Heirloom tomatoes.

and seeds to create a mixture that's about half tomato and half water. Set aside the tomato flesh for a salsa, soup, or gazpacho. A white fungus will form a layer on the surface of your pulp mixture. It signals that your mixture is ready for the next step. Stir gently and allow your seeds to sink to the bottom. Pour off the fermented pulp and tomato pieces, including any floating seeds. The viable seeds will have sunk. Rinse the seeds with water. Strain the clean seeds and spread them out on a paper plate to dry. After a few days they will be ready to store until planting. Store your seeds in a paper envelope or jar. Make sure you label them! They'll last in your house for five to seven years, or even longer if you save them in your freezer.

Some plants are easier to collect seeds from than others. Easy plants include tomatoes, peas, beans, and lettuce. These tend to self-pollinate, creating seeds that will be true to their parents.

HOST A SEED SWAP
Even if you don't garden, you can get involved by hosting a community seed swap. Invite gardeners from your community garden, local Girl Scouts, Boy Scouts, and 4-H members. Or just put a sign up in your local library. Many seed savers save more than they will plant. Invite them to bring some of their heirloom collection to share with others. Most seeds will stay viable for two to four years. Make sure your swappers know not to bring old seeds to the event. Give swappers the opportunity to bring home as many seeds as they bring to swap. You might want to supply labels and packets for the swaps. Encourage seed collectors to bring recipes that include their variety. Don't forget to include heirloom flower seeds. Donate leftover seeds to a school garden or save them for your next swap.

❦ KNOW YOUR LOCAL FARMERS

Get to know your local farmers when you visit a farmer's market. Ask them about their produce. Try a new variety! Let the farmers know what you liked when you go back.

❦ CREATE A COMPOST BIN

Set aside a large can or a plastic container in your kitchen. Ask your family to place all vegetable scraps, eggshells, and coffee grounds in the container. Take the container outside into a composting area. Cover scraps outside with leaves and grass. Stir the compost every week with a shovel. Add more scraps. After one to two months your compost will be ready to use in your garden. Mix it with soil to feed your hungry plants without adding chemicals.

❦ CREATE YOUR OWN HERBARIUM

Press samples of local species or your heirloom plants in the pages of a telephone book or between newspapers. After they dry, mount them on acid-free paper. Label your collection with date, location, and species name.

❦ COMBAT CLIMATE CHANGE

Climate change is a major factor in contributing to the loss of biodiversity. Use less energy. Limit your use of fossil fuels. Carpool. Buy items with less packaging and recycle. Using less energy is of utmost importance, but there is more that you can do. It is estimated that 17 percent of the planet's greenhouse gas emissions are generated from deforestation. Support the Lacey Act to keep the U.S. from importing illegal lumber. The Lacey Act, passed in 1900, was the first federal law that protected wildlife and the environ-

ment. Write a letter to your congressional representative in favor of upholding the Lacey Act and its 2008 amendment that prohibits U.S. companies from importing illegally forested lumber. In this way it protects foreign forests as well as our own. In the long run it will help protect our seed diversity as we attempt to control climate change. Learn about the act at www.fws.gov/international/laws-treaties-agreements/us-conservation-laws/lacey-act.html.

ADVOCATE FOR GMO LABELING

Be an informed shopper. Ask stores to label their products so that you can decide what you want to eat. Labeling puts the decision in your hands. According to a 2014 Consumer Reports finding, more than 70 percent of Americans don't want GMO ingredients in their food. As of January 2015 sixty-four countries around the world, including Europe, Japan, China, and Russia, require the labeling of genetically engineered food. If Oregon passes legislation they would be the fourth U.S. state to require labeling. Currently Vermont has passed a no-strings-attached labeling law, while Connecticut and Maine passed laws that include a trigger clause, requiring other states to pass legislation before theirs goes into effect. Check out the website Right to Know GMO: A Coalition of States for information about GMO labeling in your state.

JOIN A CSA

CSA stands for community supported agriculture. When you join, your membership fee helps a local farm buy seed and produce food for your community. You get a portion of what they grow every week. You are guaranteed to have a selection of fresh, in-season produce during the planting season each week. You might even get to try something you wouldn't ordinarily

try. Some CSAs also include flowers and other farm-grown or -produced goods. Supporting a CSA supports the farms in your community. It's a good thing for you and your local farmers.

🍎 CREATE A SCHOOL GARDEN

Get together with your classmates to plant a school garden if you don't have one already! If you do have one, volunteer to help out. Grow vegetables and fruits that might be used for your school lunches, or donate the produce to a local food pantry.

🍎 JOIN A COMMUNITY GARDEN

Grow your own veggies and flowers at your local community garden. A community garden is a great place to develop your gardening skills, because you'll be surrounded by other gardeners eager to share their knowledge with you.

🍎 CHOOSE A CAREER

If you find food and the environment something you are passionate about, think of a career that involves both! Explore an ag-career with a summer internship. Take a look at jobs in agriscience, food science, botany, and forestry.

Heirloom seeds fill the shelves at Baker Creek Seed's Petaluma Seed Bank in California.

RESOURCES

SEEDS

Not all gardens are the same. Be sure to plant seeds that will grow well in your particular climate, whether you have a southern field or a New York City rooftop garden. For example, Zach Pickens of Rooftop Ready Seeds in Brooklyn, New York, carries seeds that will do well in an environment of high wind and extreme sun exposure—perfect for urban gardens.

Check out these terrific seed companies:

Baker Creek Heirloom Seed
    Company
www.rareseeds.com

Botanical Interests
www.botanicalinterests.com

Homestead Seeds
www.the200acres.com

Hudson Valley Seed Library*
www.seedlibrary.org

John Scheeper's Kitchen Garden
    Seeds**
www.kitchengardenseeds.com

Johnny's Selected Seeds
www.johnnyseeds.com

Renee's Garden**
www.reneesgarden.com

Richmond Grows Seed Lending
    Library*
www.richmondgrowsseeds.org

Rooftop Ready Seeds
www.rooftopready.com/index

Seeds of Change**
www.seedsofchange.com

Seed Savers Exchange
www.seedsavers.org

Southern Exposure Seed Exchange
www.southernexposure.com

Sustainable Seed Company
www.sustainableseedco.com

Turtle Tree Seeds
www.turtletreeseed.org

Whillhite Seed Inc.
www.willhiteseed.com

*Seed libraries offering seeds for sale

**Seed companies offering school
    fundraiser programs

Seed libraries have sprung up across the globe. They are a free way for gardeners and farmers to exchange seeds they have saved through their local library systems. The borrower plants seeds, then saves some of the seeds at harvest time to return to the library to share with other farmers. Sounds perfect, doesn't it?

However, in some states, such as Michigan and Pennsylvania, seed libraries have been shut down by their state Department of Agriculture in violation of the Seed Act of 2004. The stipulation that the library staff must test each seed packet for germination and other requirements has prevented some libraries, such as the Joseph T. Simpson Public Library in Mechanicsburg, Pennsylvania, from accepting harvested seeds as they originally planned.

These Departments of Agriculture are concerned that seeds could be mislabeled either accidentally or intentionally, creating the spread of harmful, invasive, and poisonous plants. In an effort to curb agroterrorism, Pennsylvania's Department of Agriculture is cracking down on seed libraries throughout the state. Officials have worked with libraries, including Simpson, to encourage seed swap events.

Despite all this, there are still many that remain open across the country as lending libraries of harvested seeds. They can be a great source of seeds for your own garden. Check them out!

THE UNITED STATES

Alabama
Magnolia Springs Library
Magnolia Springs
www.magnoliaspringslibrary.org

Arizona
Pima County Public Library
Five branches in Tucson
www.library.pima.gov/seed
percent2Dlibrary

Arkansas
Faulkner County Seed Library
Conway
www.facebook.com/Faulkner-
CountySeedLibrary

California
Santa Clara Seed Share
Santa Clara
library.santaclaraca.gov/index.
aspx?page=2648

East Palo Alto Seed Library
East Palo Alto
www.collectiveroots.org/whats-
growing/community-based
-programs/east-palo-alto-seed-
library

Seed Library of Los Angeles
The Learning Garden at Venice
High School
slola.org

Yorba Linda Seed Library
Yorba Linda Public Library
Yorba Linda
ylplseedlibrary.com

Colorado
Manitou Springs Seed Library
Manitou Springs Public Library
Manitou Springs
www.manitouseedlibrary.org

Westcliffe Seed Lending Library
West Custer County Library
Westcliffe
westcliffegrows.weebly.com/index.
html

Connecticut
Fairfield Woods Seed-to-Seed
Library
Fairfield
seedlibrary.wikispaces.com/
percent2A+Home

Florida
Central Florida Seed Library
Orlando
cfsl79.wix.com/cfseedlibrary

Grow Gainesville
Highlands Presbyterian Church
growgainesville.wordpress.com/
seed-library

Hawaii
Share Seeds
Public and private spaces throughout the state
www.nomoola.com/seeds

Idaho
Common Wealth Seed Library
Boise
www.facebook.com/Common-
WealthSeedLibrary

Illinois

Chicago Seed Library
chicagoseedlibrary.org

Iowa

Barlow Seed Lending Library
Robert E. Barlow Memorial
    Library
Iowa Falls
www.iowafalls.lib.ia.us/seed-library

Ely Seed Library
Ely Public Library
www.ely.lib.ia.us/seed-lending-
    library

Louisiana

The Randle Brown Memorial Seed
    Library
Keithville
www.facebook.com/RandleBrown-
    MemorialSeedBankLibrary

Massachusetts

Concord Seed Lending Library
Concord
www.facebook.com/ConcordSeed-
    LendingLibrary

Groton Public Library Seed Lend-
    ing Library
Groton
www.gpl.org/what-we-have/seed-
    library

Michigan

Manchester District Library
Manchester
http://www.manchesterlibrary.info

Minnesota

Red River Seed Library
Moorhead

Sun Ray Library
Saint Paul
www.sppl.org/about/library-news/
    sun-ray-library-now-lending-
    seeds

Anishinaabe Seed Project
White Earth Indian Reservation
anishinaabeseedlibrary.com

Missouri

Local Harvest Seed Library
Saint Louis
thelocalharvestdish.wordpress.
    com/category/new-at-lhg

Montana

Five Valleys Seed Library
Missoula
www.facebook.com/missoulaseed-
    library

Nebraska

Common Soil Seed Library
Omaha Public Library guides.
omahalibrary.org/content.
php?pid=111386&sid=
3563743

New Hampshire

Hooksett Seed Lending Library
www.hooksettlibrary.org/services/
seed-lending-library

New Jersey

Catherine Dickson Hofman Seed
Library
Warren County Library
www1.youseemore.com/warrencl/
contentpages.asp?loc=101

New Mexico

Seed Broadcast Mobile Seed
Library
Anton Chico
www.seedbroadcast.org/Seed
Broadcast/SeedBroadcast.html

New York

Urban Seed Library
New York City
www.facebook.com/UrbanSeed
Library

Pine Plains Seed Library
Pine Plains Free Library
www.facebook.com/PinePlains
SeedLibrary

North Carolina

Sylva Sprouts Seed Lending
Library

Jackson County
jacksoncountyfarmersmarket.org/
sylva-sprouts-seed-lending-
library-2

Ohio

Cleveland Seed Library
Cleveland Public Library
Branches — six branches
www.clevelandseedbank.org/events

Oregon

Coquille Valley Seed Library
coquillevalleyseedlibrary.org

Green Lents Seed Library
Portland
www.greenlents.org/green-lents-
seed-library-ready-for-
donations

Portland Seed Library
portlandseedlibrary.net

Pennsylvania

Philadelphia Seed Exchange
phillyseedexchange.wordpress.com

Pittsburgh Seed and Story Library
Lawrenceville branch of Carnegie
Library of Pittsburgh
www.facebook.com/seedand
storypgh

Texas

Sustainable Food Center
Austin
www.sustainablefoodcenter.org

Vermont

Windsor Public Library
windsorlibrary.org/services/seed-
library

Virginia

Seed Lending Library
Abingdon
www.facebook.com/pages/
Seed-Lending-
Library/473389989376845

Goochland Campus Library
Reynolds Community College
jsrcclibrary.wordpress.
com/2013/03/14/goochland-
library-hosts-seed-library

Washington

Olympia Seed Exchange
www.olympiaseedexchange.org

West Virginia

Summers County Public Library
Hinton
summers.lib.wv.us/seedlending
library.htm

Wisconsin

Green Lake Seed Library
Green Lake Library
www.facebook.com/pages/
Green-Lake-Seed-
Library/569494099737128

Walworth County Seed Library
Lake Geneva
www.walworthseedlibrary.org

OUTSIDE THE UNITED STATES

Berlin Seed Library

Germany
www.facebook.com/BerlinSeed
Library

Seed Guardians Seed Library

Slovenia
www.semenska.org/the-seed-
library.html

London Seed Library

England
www.facebook.com/
pages/London-Seed-
Library/148520191979439

Semilla Besada Seed Library

Granada, Spain
www.holisticdecisions.com

Toronto Seed Library

Canada
www.torontoseedlibrary.org

ADDITIONAL RESOURCES

ORGANIZATIONS

United States Patent and Trademark Office Overview of Plant Patents:
www.uspto.gov/web/offices/pac/plant/#1

Locate your nearest community garden and find gardening tips at the American Community Gardening Association:
www.communitygarden.org

Learn more about creating and maintaining a school garden through the National Gardening Association:
www.kidsgardening.org/node/120

Right to Know GMO: A Coalition of States:
righttoknow-gmo.org

Seed Freedom:
seedfreedom.info

Sign Dr. Vandana Shiva's Declaration on Seed Freedom:
seedfreedom.in/declaration navdanya.org

Learn about heritage foods at Slow Food USA:
slowfoodusa.org

March Against Monsanto:
march-against-monsanto.com

Learn more about careers in botany:
www.botany.org/bsa/careers

WATCH

Bitter Seeds. Directed by Micha Peled. San Francisco. Teddy Bear Films, 2011. DVD.

Dirt! The Movie. Directed by Bill Benenson and Gene Rosow. Santa Monica. Common Ground Media, 2009. DVD.

"In Vavilov's Footsteps: A Documentary." YouTube video. Directed by Nicoletta Fagiolo. Uploaded February 14, 2011. www.youtube.com/watch?v=y2dPObz2Bsc.

"Two Options." Vimeo video, interview with Dr. Shiva and Bija Devi.

Created by the Perennial Plate. October 2013. vimeo.com/59404290.

"The Vavilov Institute." National Geographic video. 2011. natgeotv.com/asia/seed-hunter/videos/the-vavilov-institute.

PBS. Gardens of the World. 1993. Narrated by Audrey Hepburn, See trailer at www.youtube.com/watch?v=t6ArElsvCUA www.gardensoftheworld.org

READ

Bartoletti, Susan Campbell. *Black Potatoes: The Story of the Great Irish Famine, 1845–1850.* Boston: Houghton Mifflin, 2001.

Burleigh, Robert. *Chocolate: Riches from the Rainforest,* NY: Harry N. Abrams, 2002.

Chevat, Richie, and Michael Pollan. *The Omnivore's Dilemma: The Secrets Behind What You Eat,* Young Readers Edition. New York: Dial, 2009:

Frydenborg, Kay. *Chocolate: Sweet Science and Dark Secrets of the World's Favorite Treat.* Boston: Houghton Mifflin, 2015.

Gibbons, Gail. *Corn.* NY: Holiday House, 2008.

Schlosser, Eric, and Charles Wilson. *Chew on This: The Unhappy Truth About Fast Food.* Boston: Houghton Mifflin, 2006.

VISIT

The World Carrot Museum. Berlotte, Belgium. carrotmuseum.co.uk

National Mustard Museum. Wisconsin, USA. mustardmuseum.com

National Apple Museum. Biglerville, PA, USA. nationalapplemuseum.com

The Farmer's Museum. Cooperstown, N.Y., USA. farmersmuseum.org

National Heirloom Expo. Annually Santa Rosa, Calif., USA. theheirloomexpo.com

Luther Burbank Home and Gardens. Santa Rosa, Calif., USA. lutherburbank.org

KEW Gardens/Royal Botanical Gardens. Surrey, England. kew.org

GLOSSARY

Agronomist—An expert in soil governance and agriculture production.

Alleles—Multiple forms of genes on a chromosome.

Biopiracy—The theft of wild or indigenous plants by corporations that then patent them for their own profit.

Blight—A plant disease that is often caused by fungi, including mildews, rusts, and smuts.

Botany—The scientific study of plants.

Corn Belt—A region in the American Midwest that is excellent for growing corn and raising livestock. It includes the states of Illinois, Iowa, and Indiana.

Cross-pollinate—To transfer pollen to one flower from another variety; its seed then is a mixture of both parents.

Heirloom—An open-pollinated variety that has been around for about fifty or more years and is shared within a community or family.

Herbicide—A chemical or substance that is lethal to plants and is used to control unwanted vegetation.

Hybrid—First- or second-generation cross of inbred parent lines. Offspring seeds will not exhibit the traits of the parents, or breed true. Instead, they will take on some or none of their genetic traits; e.g., a poodle and a golden retriever will not produce a poodle. They will produce a Goldendoodle.

Genetically engineered (GE) or genetically modified (GM)—Artificially created varieties formed by scientifically altering the genetic makeup of the variety.

Landrace—A local variety of domesticated plant (or animal) species that has been developed over time by its environment.

Monoculture—The cultivation of a single crop.

Open-pollination—Pollination that occurs by an insect, bird, wind, or other natural mechanism, leading to a very diverse community of plants.

Pathogen—Virus, bacterium, or fungus that causes disease.

Pesticides—substances kill pests. Pesticides include herbicides and insecticides.

Seed—A seed or kernel houses a fertilized plant ovule that contains a tiny embryonic plant and nutrition, and is covered by a seed coat for protection.

Self-pollinate—To transfer pollen from the anther to the stigma in the same flower.

Summer Hunger—The period of July and August when the last season's crop was finished and before the new crop was ready to pick.

AUTHOR'S NOTE

The path for this book has been long and well traveled. I started out loving a tiny little Whitman book titled *What Shall I Put in the Hole That I Dig?* when I was just a toddler. During that time in my life I can remember being with my grandfather in his garden, standing among plants that were taller than me. Like many of the people in this book I grew up eating homegrown tomatoes and other vegetables. And I watched the corn grow high in nearby fields.

Between writing books on oceans, deserts, and rainforests, I wrote an article about gardening with kids, but it wasn't until I wrote *Keeping Our Earth Green* and my daughter began working at a local farm store that I realized we were deep into a seed crisis. How could I have taken my food for granted all this time?

Researching *The Story of Seeds* was both challenging and rewarding. It was challenging because I was dependent on weather for many of the photographs. Plants don't go to seed every week of the year. In addition, the United States government shut down! That's right. Just as I was planning a trip to our U.S. seed vault in Iowa, it closed along with every other U.S. facility. That left me with my trip planned to Russia in the dead of winter! Who goes to Russia at the end of January to talk plants and seeds? I did! It was a blessing in disguise. I was certainly not in tourist season and I was able to experience the harshness and cold of a Russian winter just as the scientists did during the Leningrad siege.

That leads me to the rewards — there were many! I was figuring out how to interview Dr. Vandana Shiva when I learned she was speaking an hour away from me two days later! Talk about luck! I had the same serendipitous event in locating Dr. Cary Fowler to interview him. It seemed as if everything was aligning for this book. I was able to meet many of the seed defenders at the National Heirloom Expo in California. And the expo was held near the home of Luther Burbank — it was perfect!

Every challenge seemed to lead me along a path to another reward.

Each one of the seed defenders I encountered while writing this book, so many I couldn't include them all, has put an indelible mark on my soul. Their passion, humility, and persistence have had a great impact on me.

Whether I was meeting them on their family farm, in an orchard, across the country or across continents, they opened me up to new ideas and new ways of thinking about our earth. I am eternally grateful to them all, and I couldn't wait to share the stories of researching this book with my readers.

In addition, I'd like to thank my family, who traveled along the path with me, even to Russia, and my writer buddies, Anita Sanchez, Lois Huey, Rose Kent, Helen Mesick, Liza Frenette, and Kyra Teis. And it wouldn't have come together at all without the persistence and enthusiasm of my editor, Erica Zappy, the hardworking team at Houghton Mifflin Harcourt, and my agent, Jennifer Laughran.

I hope that in writing this book I have joined in the bucket brigade of which Dr. Cary Fowler so eloquently spoke.

125

SOURCES

"All About Chocolate—the Cacao Tree." Accessed December 24, 2013. www.xocoatl.org

"Arctic 'Doomsday' Seed Vault Opens Doors for 100 Million Seeds." *ScienceDaily*. February 27, 2008. www.sciencedaily.com/releases/2008/02/080226092753.htm.

Bardoe, Cheryl, and Joseph A. Smith. *Gregor Mendel: The Friar Who Grew Peas.* New York: Abrams for Young Readers, 2006.

Barsamian, David. "Vandana Shiva." *Progressive* 61, no. 9 (September 1997): 36.

Basra, Amarjit S. *Handbook of Seed Science and Technology.* New York: Food Products, 2006.

Bateson, Patrick. "William Bateson: A Biologist Ahead of His Time." *Journal of Genetics* 81, no. 2 (2002): 49–59. www.ias.ac.in/gen/vol81No2/49.pdf.

Berry, Thomas. *The Dream of the Earth.* San Francisco: Sierra Club, 1988.

Bewley, J. Derek, Michael Black, and P. Halmer. *The Encyclopedia of Seeds: Science, Technology and Uses.* Wallingford, UK: CABI, 2006.

Beyers, Becky. "Building a Better Potato." *Solutions: College of Food, Agricultural and Natural Resource Sciences* (Winter 2009): 8–11.

"Biotechnology." National Agricultural Law Center. Accessed January 7, 2014. Nationalaglawcenter.org/overview/biotechnology-overview.

"The BT Cotton Suicide Belt." GM-Free Cymru. Accessed February 27, 2013.

Caldas, M. M., and S. Perz. "Agro-Terrorism? The Causes and Consequences of the Appearance of Witch's Broom Disease in Cocoa Plantations of Southern Bahia, Brazil." *Journal-Geoforum* 47 (2013): 147–57. krex.ksu.edu. krex.k-state.edu/dspace/handle/2097/16756.

"Cary Fowler: One Seed at a Time, Protecting the Future of Food." July 2009. TED video. Posted February 27, 2013. www.ted.com/talks/cary_fowler_one_seed_at_a_time_protecting_the_future_of_food?language=en

Charles, Dan. "A Tale of Two Seed Farmers: Organic vs. Engineered." NPR. January 24, 2011. www.npr.org/2011/01/25/1333178893/a-tale-of-two-seed-farmers-organic-vs-engineered.

"A Conversation with Vandana Shiva—Question 6—Seeds as the Spinning Wheel of Today." February 26, 2012. YouTube video. www.youtube.com/watch?v=ub2ruF10K_w.

Copeland, L. O. *Principles of Seed Science and Technology.* Minneapolis: Burgess, 1976.

Crow, J. F. "NI Vavilov, Martyr to Genetic Truth." *Genetics* 134, no. 1 (1993): 1.

———. "Plant Breeding Giants: Burbank, the Artist; Vavilov, the Scientist." *Genetics* 158, no. 4 (2001): 1391–95.

Cuevas, Flavio A. "Day of Native Corn—Oaxaca, Mexico." *Seed Freedom.* September 2013. Seedfreedom.in/day-of-native-corn-oaxaca-mexico.

Cummings, Claire Hope. *Uncertain Peril: Genetic Engineering and the Future of Seeds.* Boston: Beacon, 2008.

Deane-Drummond, Celia. *Eco-theology.* London: Darton, Longman and Todd, 2008.

Dirt! The Movie. Directed by Bill Benenson and Gene Rosow. DVD. 2009. Common Ground Media. Santa Monica, CA.

"'Doomsday' Seed Vault to Open in Norway." CNN. www.cnn.com/2008/WORLD/europe/20/25/norway.seeds/index.html.

Edelson, Edward. *Gregor Mendel: And the Roots of Genetics.* New York: Oxford University Press, 1999.

Engdahl, Frederick William. *Seeds of Destruction: The Hidden Agenda of Genetic Manipulation.* Montreal: Global Research, 2007.

Fowler, Cary, and Pat Mooney. *Shattering: Food, Politics, and the Loss of Genetic Diversity.* Tucson: University of Arizona Press, 1990.

Gettle, Jere. Personal interview. September 12, 2013.

Gillis, Justin. "Temperature Rising: A Warming Planet Struggles to Feed Itself." *New York Times.* June 5, 2011. www.nytimes.com/2011/06/05/science/earth/05harvest.html.

"Global Crop Diversity Trust." Global Crop Diversity Trust. Accessed January 10, 2012. www.croptrust.org.

Gordon, Susan. *Critical Perspectives on Genetically Modified Crops and Food.* New York: Rosen, 2006.

Gribbin, John. *Forecasts, Famines, and Freezes: Climate and Man's Future.* New York: Walker, 1976.

Henig, Robin Marantz. *The Monk in the Garden: The Lost and Found Genius of Gregor Mendel, the Father of Genetics.* Boston: Houghton Mifflin Harcourt 2000.

Hildebrand, J. R. "Revolution in Eating." *National Geographic* 81, no. 3 (1942): 273–322.

Illirk, Sarah. "Bitch In: Red River Seed Library." *Bitch.* Winter 2014, 8–9.

Jacobs, Paul. "A Few Rush to Exploit New Biotech Crops." *Los Angeles Times.*
December 31, 1999.

Kloppenburg, Jack Ralph. *Seeds and Sovereignty: The Use and Control of Plant Genetic Resources.* Durham, NC: Duke University Press, 1988.

Loskutov, Igor G. Interview with the author. January 20, 2014.

———. *Vavilov and His Institute.* Rome: International Plant Genetic Resources Institute, 1999.

Mendel, Gregor. "Versuche über Plflanzenhybriden." *Verhand- lungen des natur- forschenden Vereines in Brünn, Bd. IV für das Jahr 1865,* Abhandlungen, 1866: 3–47. Experiments in Plant Hybridization. www.esp.org/foundations/ genetics/classical/gm-65.pdf.

Makarov, Boris. Interview with the author. January 20, 2014.

Moyer, Michael. "Death and Chocolate: Disease Threatens to Devastate Global Cocoa Supply." *Scientific American.* 2010.

Nabhan, Gary Paul. *Where Our Food Comes From: Retracing Nikolay Vavilov's Quest to End Famine.* Washington, DC: Island/Shearwater, 2009.

Opar, Alisa. "Food Culture." *Audubon.* March 2011, 87–89.

Pearce, Fred. "The Great Seed Blitzkrieg." *New Scientist.* January 5, 2008, 2–5.

Penn State. "Finest Chocolate May Get Better: Cacao Tree Genome Sequenced." *ScienceDaily.* December 28, 2010. news.psu.edu/story/161954/2010/12/26/ food-gods-genome-sequence-could-make-finest-chocolate-better.

Popovsky, Mark. "The Last Days of Nikolai Vavilov." *New Scientist.* November 16, 1978, 509–10.

Pringle, Peter. *Food, Inc.: Mendel to Monsanto — the Promises and Perils of the Biotech Harvest.* New York: Simon & Schuster, 2003.

———. *The Murder of Nikolai Vavilov: The Story of Stalin's Persecution of One of the Great Scientists of the Twentieth Century.* New York: Simon & Schuster, 2008.

Robin, Marie-Monique. *The World According to Monsanto: Pollution, Corruption, and the Control of the World's Food Supply.* New York: New Press, 2010.

Rosenthal, Elisabeth. "In the Fields of Italy, a Conflict over Corn." *New York Times.* August 23, 2010.

"Safeguarding the Future of US Agriculture: The Need to Conserve Threatened Collections of Crop Diversity Worldwide." www.croptrust.org/documents/ WEBpdf/TrustReportfinal.pdf.

Sample, Ian. "Palm Tree Grown from 2,000-Year-Old Date Stone." *Guardian.* June 12, 2008. www.theguardian.com/science/2008/jun12/ancient.seed.

Sauer, Carl Ortwin. *Agricultural Origins and Dispersals.* New York: American Geographical Society, 1952.

Schoen, Greg. "The Origins and Journey of 'Carl's Glass Gems' Rainbow Corn." *Mother Earth News.* December 13, 2012. www.motherearthnews.com/homesteading-and-livestock/glass-corn-seed-zwfz1212zrob.asphax223 GgjSIDOH.

Secretariat of the Convention on Biological Diversity. *Biodiversity and Agriculture: Safeguarding Biodiversity and Securing Food for the World.* May 22, 2008. World Trade Center, Montreal, Quebec. http://www.seedlibrarian.com.

"Seeds: Regional Seed Banks." This Is Fertile Ground. Accessed February 27, 2013.

Shiva, Vandana. "The Basmati Battle and Its Implications for Biopiracy and Trips." Center for Research on Globalization. Accessed September 10, 2001. Globalresearch.ca/articles/SH1209A.html.

———. Interview with the author. September 11, 2013.

———. "Making Peace with the Earth: Shifting to Feminist Economics, Politics, and Culture." Lecture. A Day with Vandana Shiva. Vassar College, Poughkeepsie, NY. March 6, 2013.

———. *Manifestos on the Future of Food & Seed.* Cambridge, MA: South End, 2007.

Singer, Emily. "A Comeback for Lamarckian Evolution?" *MIT Technology Review.* February 4, 2009. www.technologyreview.com/news/411880/a-comeback-for-Lamarckian-Evolution.

Smekalova, Tamara. Interview with the author. January 20, 2014.

Solowey, Elaine. Email interview with the author. October 18, 2013.

"Songs of the Mandan and Hidatsa." Recorded and edited by Frances Densmore. Accessed December 22, 2013. www.drumhop.com.

Stein, Lori, and Bonnie L. Webber. "Farmers Fight Back, Challenge Monsanto over Patents for Its Transgenic Seeds." *Sierra Atlantic* 39 (2012): 8.

Thomson, Jennifer A. *Seeds for the Future: The Impact of Genetically Modified Crops on the Environment.* Ithaca, NY: Comstock, 2007.

Verjuk, Vladimir. Interview with the author. January 20, 2014.

Weaver, William Woys. *Heirloom Vegetable Gardening: A Master Gardener's Guide to Planting, Growing, Seed Saving, and Cultural History.* New York: Henry Holt, 1997.

Weaver, William Woys. Lecture. National Heirloom Expo. September, 2013.

Wong, Edward. "Good Earth Gone: Polluted Soil Plagues China." *New York Times.* December 30, 2013.

TIMELINE

1822   Gregor Mendel is born.

1845   The Great Hunger begins in Ireland.

1865   Mendel publishes the results of his pea experiments.

1868   Darwin publishes *Variations of Animals and Plants Under Domestication.*

1873   Luther Burbank attempts to create a new potato—the Burbank potato.

1907   Luther Burbank begins work on developing spineless cacti.

1916   Nikolai Vavilov heads off on his first seed-gathering expedition.

1926   Vavilov publishes *Origin of Geography of Cultivated Plants.* Luther Burbank dies.

1931   The first plant patent is given to Henry Boseberg.

1934   Drought begins to set off the Dust Bowl environmental disaster.

1940   J. I. Rodale and his wife purchase a farm to raise food for his family using the "organic" method described by Sir Albert Howard. Vavilov is arrested.

1941   Lenigrad seige begins—Hitler advances on Vavilov Institute.

1942   The Russian scientist Alexander Shchukin dies of starvation inside the Vavilov Institute. Others follow. *Organic Farming and Gardening Magazine* debuts.

1944   The Leningrad Seige ends.

1950   U.S. Congress passes HR 323 authorizing an investigation of chemical fertilizers and poison sprays.

1952   The famous actress Gloria Swanson warns against arsenic-sprayed produce.

1962   Rachel Carson's *A Silent Spring* is serialized, then published in book form.

1969   A corn blight hits America.

1970	The first Earth Day is held.
1983	Sibella Kraus plans Tasting of the Summer Produce.
1989	The actress Meryl Streep testifies in Washington, D.C., against pesticide use.
1990	Congress passes the Organic Foods Production Act, setting national organic labeling standards.
1992	The USDA appoints the first National Organic Standards Board.
1996	The Iraqi black box of seeds is smuggled out of Iraq.
	William Weaver publishes *Heirloom Vegetable Gardening* and appears on *Good Morning America*.
	Monsanto introduces herbicide-resistant corn.
1997	The Favr Savr tomato is genetically engineered.
1999	Unilever and Nestle halt the use of genetically engineered ingredients in European product lines.
2001	A national genetic labeling law fails in the U.S. Congress.
2002	Afghanistan's seed vault is looted.
2003	Dr. Sanaa Abdul Wahab El Sheikh saves precious Iraqi seeds during war.
2004	The Hudson Valley Seed Library is founded.
2008	The Svalbard Global Seed Vault opens in Norway.
	Monsanto deploys Roundup Ready products.
2011	Herbicide-resistant corn is grown in fourteen countries.
2012	Monsanto threatens to sue states that pass GMO labeling legislation.
	California fails to pass a GMO labeling law.
2013	Eight hundred farmer's markets operate in California.
	Maine and Connecticut pass a GMO labeling law but require other states to pass laws before theirs goes into effect.
	Monsanto expected 39 to 41 million soybean acres to be planted with Roundup Ready Soybeans.
2014	Vermont passes a GMO labeling law.
	It is Earth's warmest year on record.

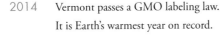

INDEX